TENANT'S SURVIVAL GUIDE

Lesley Henderson has been a landlord all her adult life and now runs a family business. She is married with four children and lives in Surrey.

TENANT'S SURVIVAL GUIDE

LESLEY HENDERSON

ROBERT HALE · LONDON

© *Lesley Henderson 1999*
First published in Great Britain 1999

ISBN 0 7090 6529 9

Robert Hale Limited
Clerkenwell House
Clerkenwell Green
London EC1R 0HT

2 4 6 8 10 9 7 5 3 1

Typeset in North Wales by
Derek Doyle and Associates, Mold, Flintshire.
Printed in Great Britain by
St Edmundsbury Press Limited, Bury St Edmunds
and bound by
WBC Book Manufacturers Limited, Bridgend

Contents

Preface

Having worked in the lettings industry for most of my adult life, I have become keenly aware that practical information for tenants is obviously not circulating very efficiently.

I can think of no industry or service equivalent to the rental sector, despite its importance and its economic significance. Far from being a major service provider like, for example, a large manufacturing company, where regulations are relatively easy to enforce, the rental industry is made up of thousands of individual providers, each with a relatively small number of units; making it both difficult and costly to regulate.

There are now, particularly since the introduction of the Housing Acts 1988, a huge number of agencies and private landlords offering property; but tenants have little understanding of what they should expect, nor what is expected of them in exchange for their rent. Both good and bad practice is widespread, and tenants with little experience have nothing consistent to base their choices upon.

The increase in the number of agents setting up over the last ten years can only be described as phenomenal. Tenants must now negotiate with these 'brokers', and often never even meet the landlord with whom they have a contract, or indeed a legitimate dispute.

Rising student numbers have massively increased

demand at the lower end of the price range in every university town, and a recent Appeal Court decision has effectively removed some of the basic safety protection from this large number of tenants, who have always rented in groups for economy.

Although it is often believed and stated that tenants have rights under a variety of Housing Acts, common law, and Consumer Protection Acts, in reality this protection is about as much use as a chocolate teapot for anyone with six months' security of tenure under an Assured Shorthold lease. By the time any action can be taken to enforce safety or contract, the landlord may very well have refused to extend the complaining tenant's lease.

By providing information that can be easily understood and related to, this guide should help you to search with a good idea of what to look for, conduct your tenancy in a manner which is unlikely to be problematic, and with luck, leave with your deposit intact. The guide is not intended to be a legal manual, but a practical one – for when the law is of as little effective use as it is for the vast majority of tenants, practicality rather than theory is what will help you most.

Introduction

Brief outline

Over the past decade, there has been an unprecedented range of changes to Housing Law. The most significant of these changes has undoubtedly been the introduction in 1988 of assured shorthold leases. Until their introduction, almost all tenancies required a landlord to prove (in court if required) that s/he had good enough legal reasons for requiring the tenancy to be terminated. The introduction of these new tenancies means that any landlord who decides to terminate a tenancy after a short period may do so. There is no longer any requirement to prove that the tenant has breached a term of the lease. Leases granted in this way may therefore be terminated for no legal reason whatsoever. Tenants have no control, once the 'fixed term' has expired, over the length of time they will be able to continue their contract. Together with other far-reaching changes, this legislation has utterly transformed the lettings industry.

This transformation has had both hugely positive and hugely negative effects. There has been a genuine upturn in the supply of rented housing. Previously the supply was patchy and inadequate, and the return of investors to this sector has been of huge benefit to everyone who needs to rent accommodation. Gone are the days when the supply of accommodation was very limited, and nowadays, when higher education and shorter-term employment contracts mean we all have to move around much more than we ever did before, this increased supply is absolutely vital.

However, whilst everyone welcomes the increased supply and choice, gone also are the days when tenancies lasted for as long as the tenant wanted, so long as the terms were not breached. The whole way in which we occupy rented property has changed beyond recognition over the past decade. 'Market rents' have replaced 'fair rents', which at least offered some control on costs. Tight contracts, in which every detail of tenant conduct is clearly laid out, are now far more commonplace. Agencies have been rapidly established to service this growing sector. Being a tenant is now more costly and less secure than it has been for decades. These changes affect every single aspect of being a tenant.

What difference does this make to me?

The first difference this has made is that if you do want to be a tenant, you will have no difficulty in becoming one. This may seem obvious, but for many years, due to the previous legislation, the supply of rented accommodation almost dried up.

However, the climate in which you occupy has been utterly transformed. Until the changes in the Housing Acts 1988, tenants enjoyed almost unlimited security of tenure. The introduction of assured shorthold leases has removed that security. Landlords may offer this type of lease with no obligation to extend it, as they enjoy an automatic right of possession after six months. This one fact alone has restricted tenants enormously. Every player – landlords, agents and tenants – now knows, that if tenants complain, their lease need not last beyond the legal minimum, and this is usually only six months.

The difference that this has made is absolutely critical. Tenants now enter a highly commercialized, expensive market, in the certain knowledge that if they have even the most reasonable cause for complaint, they may, for no other reason than raising a problem, be asked to leave their home. We have entered unchartered waters where tenants even with very real problems with their accommodation do not feel confident enough to complain.

It is very easy for people who are not directly affected to shrug their shoulders, and wonder why you should mind moving on if you're not happy. Moving is expensive, and traumatic, whether you're a tenant or a home owner. It is however doubly ironic that your single largest expense, i.e. your home, should be the one thing that you are unable to raise any legitimate concerns about. I know of one young couple who lived for four months with a broken cooker because their agent made it clear that the landlord would not renew their lease if any repair accounts were submitted, 'on principle'!

The Housing Acts 1988 may have solved the problems of under-supply, but they have in reality created another, quite different set of problems. Interestingly, problems in the seventies and eighties were genuinely experienced by landlords, who even when they had the most appalling problems with their tenants found it almost impossible to regain possession of their property. A completely different type of problem now exists, this time for tenants who, despite paying high rents, and signing very stringent contracts, find it is their turn to be relatively powerless.

What should I do to protect my interests?

In this highly commercial market, where rights are

limited, tenants need to know what to look for, not only in the property itself, but also in its management (agent or landlord). Ideally tenants need to be well informed before they ever sign a contract. Inexperienced tenants (and they form the majority) need to learn how to assess and protect their own interests quickly and efficiently. Property is now very expensive to rent – it can easily consume half your disposable income – and good units go very quickly in a market where they are still at a premium. Learning what to look for and why is now an essential part of being a tenant.

How will the *Tenant's Survival Guide* help me?

The aim of the guide is primarily to educate tenants, whilst simultaneously building a sensible framework within which both you and your landlord can operate. It sets out not only what you can expect from your landlord or agent, but also what they can reasonably expect from you. It will warn you about common pitfalls, and give advice on how to avoid them. It will help you to recognize what should concern you, and show you some easy, practical ways to protect your own interests.

You may find some of the guide alarming, some of it amusing, but all of it will help you negotiate the realities of being a private tenant today. Throughout the guide you will find numerous anecdotes from landlords and tenants, which have been used to illustrate potential pitfalls. Given that all of us learn best from experience, you will find them very useful. These will enable you to learn from the past misfortunes of others (there's no substitute for experience, even if it's someone else's!). None of these is invented, and they have been included as illustrations of inexperience.

What is in this *Tenant's Survival Guide*?

Most local authorities, Citizens' Advice Bureaux and tenancy advisory groups have already produced small, quite helpful pamphlets for tenants. They do however tend to concentrate on clear areas like major disrepair (the roof fell in), illegal eviction (suitcases in the front garden), and other forms of major harassment. Many also still include information on tenancies which are no longer likely to be issued, as these booklets are intended to cover the whole spectrum of tenancy problems and there are still a surprising number of regulated tenants with old contracts that are still running.

The *Tenant's Survival Guide* does not seek to travel down this already well-documented path. It is designed quite specifically to cover only lease types for Assured Shorthold tenants, or those who have been offered 'licences to occupy'. It is able therefore to concentrate on the tenant with little or no security of tenure and very few rights to enforce. Very often, despite their being in the overwhelming majority of recent tenancies, problem-solving advice for this huge and growing army of tenants is usually brief. It is often also accompanied by a warning that you have very little security, and you might not want to enforce the limited rights you do have. Fewer rights mean that you need to know how to *avoid* problems because you will never be in a position to force anyone to rectify them.

One of the reasons I suspect for the lack of available advice is that, whilst tenants' groups and services have fought for tenant rights in older-style tenancies with considerable success, the same rights simply do not apply to the newer tenancies. It is much harder to advise people when they have very little legal redress. If you complain, or have a problem with your landlord on an assured shorthold, and that lease is legitimately brought to an end by your landlord, what has happened may be grossly unfair, but it is certainly not illegal!

Put simply, informed tenants will do well, and badly informed tenants will not. Landlords and agents have quickly learned how to manage uninformed tenants. The purpose of this guide is to place in the hands of tenants the same range of experience as that held by the other parties to the contract. This guide gives you the information you need to function in the same way. Longer than a pamphlet (but shorter than *War and Peace*), this guide aims to help you both foresee and resolve the type of problems you are likely to be dealing with as a tenant with limited tenure, whilst taking very little of your time to read. The book is a practical guide that every tenant needs to read to get a feeling for being a tenant, and of how the industry works in practical terms. It is also a technical reference point which enables you to look up specific details about your own tenancy, or specific less common matters either before you sign your contract, or should a problem arise during your tenancy.

Where else could I get advice?

It has been remarkably difficult for tenants to actually get hold of useful advice about these types of tenancies, which is why this guide has been written. The usual sources, where anyone would normally try first, would be friends and family, especially when embarking upon something so expensive and laden with problems as renting property. However, the advice of family, friends, etc., is in this instance usually of little real help. Very often the advice on assured shortholds is limited; because your *rights* are limited. There's nothing else to say! These particular tenancies need 'management'. You need to be forewarned about their knock-on effects, and advised about their consequences, because you certainly can't exercise control over them. The enormous range of changes, which have so transformed the market, have created circumstances and problems about which anyone who was a tenant in, say, the seventies and early eighties, would be completely unable to understand, e.g. little security of tenure, very short contracts, agency practices, etc.

In many parts of Europe, where renting has always been a majority lifestyle, moving out of home would mean simply exchanging one similar tenancy type for another. In Britain, this is not the case, and the normal base of experience is unavailable. In addition, given our national preference for home ownership, being a tenant is usually transitional; something we do for a relatively short time before we buy a house. We therefore have no real way of accumulating experience.

The law is also relatively young, and is itself changing through legal decisions on a fairly regular basis. Finding out what you need to know is therefore far more difficult than taking advice about a pension, a car, or a house purchase, where advice is plentiful.

The majority of press coverage is dedicated to the problems which landlords face, or the investment opportunities available in this emergent industry, seemingly leaving tenants to hope for the best. The only other readily available source of information which tenants can access is legal advice. However, most of us (except in the most serious of instances) find this a very expensive option. Too often tenants realize that their position is insecure, and that their landlord is holding a considerable sum of *their* money. For many, it is simply cheaper to cut their losses than to spend more money fighting a battle which in many cases they doubt they can win.

Final Advice

Many landlords are excellent, providing high quality, safe and well-serviced properties; some landlords are appalling, offering inadequate, overcrowded, and sometimes downright unsafe properties which should never be available; and the overwhelming majority fall, as in all other walks of life, somewhere between the two.

Don't however forget that even if it often doesn't feel that way, you are a *customer* of your landlord. It may be your rent which will be paying the mortgage on this property, perhaps whilst they are abroad. Your landlord may be acquiring a portfolio of properties, all funded by rental income. You may not have too many legal remedies available to you, but landlords and agencies cannot survive without tenants' revenue, which funds the entire industry. A contract between two parties based on mutual respect for the other's role has a much greater chance of success.

As a tenant, rent is likely to be your single largest expense this year; far more costly than, for example, your car payments. This guide should equip you well in your search for accommodation. Landlords and agents are well prepared – you need to ensure that they aren't the only parties who know what they are doing!

1 Rental Valuations

Landlords and agencies are, since the introduction of the Housing Acts 1988, allowed to charge the 'going rate' for rented accommodation for all tenancies granted since its introduction. This is known as the 'market rent' as opposed to the old 'fair rents' that applied before. Most of us should welcome this. Fair rents contributed to the sharp decline in property to rent, and potential investors are now encouraged to buy property to let out. Previously, despite rapidly rising housing prices, any tenant could apply to have a fair rent registered on their accommodation. This could easily mean that landlords had rent levels legally set which meant that they couldn't even cover their costs. Small wonder that no new properties were coming on the market.

There are still some very limited facilities which tenants can use, but only in situations where they really believe that the rent they are being charged is basically outrageous. Rent Assessment Committees exist to exert limits on totally unreasonable rent levels; but tenants should be very wary about making an application. Very often rent levels are raised by this committee. If you genuinely feel that the rent you are being charged is totally out of line with others in the same area, you can obtain details from your citizens' advice bureau about where your local R.A.C. is. Check thoroughly before you make an application. All R.A.C.s keep a public record of their decisions, which you can check. If the difference is marginal they are unlikely to intervene, and you are likely to have irritated your landlord for no good reason.

Far better than taking on a property which you think is unreasonably priced, or worse still, one that you are going to have difficulty managing to pay for, is to look carefully at what is on offer generally in the area you need, and rent something which you can afford. There are two alternative places to search.

The local lettings agencies

Most towns are now awash with lettings agents (estate agents who do lettings) and accommodation agencies. A quick walk down any High Street, or a brief scan through any local paper will show you just how many there are. Every one of them has property on their books and is looking for tenants. But *beware*: all agents have many additional fees of which inexperienced tenants may not even be aware.

> Agents are forbidden by law from charging tenants for simply providing lists of available accommodation. We are hearing stories however that some London agencies are trying to charge a fee to *show* you a property. If someone asks you for seventy-five pounds to see a flat, find another agency!

Finding accommodation through agents can have some unexpected costs. Agents usually charge prospective tenants for taking up references, which is reasonable. However, they are usually requesting two or three, at a cost of about twenty pounds each. If, for example, they need two references from each of four sharing tenants, a considerable sum of money will be needed. Some charge an additional fee on each actual let.

Some agents have a number of tenants, or groups of tenants, interested in renting a particular property. This is understandably more likely the nicer the property. Do make sure that you are not in some kind of race, where a number of potential tenants are each being charged for references, but only one will be successful. Ask the agent to confirm *before* you agree to pay if anyone else is being considered for the property, or if they are already taking up references on anyone else's behalf. Several interested groups all being referenced simultaneously can be very profitable for agencies.

Agencies usually charge tenants a 'lease signing fee'. It may be known by another term, but basically it is a charge for signing the lease. The cost of these vary but it may be around seventy-five pounds. Do ensure that if at all possible you insist that the length of the lease ('fixed terms' are most common with agencies) is as long as you are likely to need. Many agents offer six months initially, and then recharge the same tenants each time a least extension or a new lease is offered. These fees are very expensive, and are usually explained away by general reference to 'administration' costs. They can hit students (who usually need at least a nine-month tenancy term) very hard, especially if they are unexpected. Try (it is not easy) to negotiate *at this initial stage* the first fixed term for the length of time you are most likely to need it, to save later 'administration' fees. For a number of reasons, not all of them financial, which will become clearer as you read your guide, it is always preferable to have the full term you require on your initial lease, so long as you are quite sure you will not want or need to move out earlier.

Agencies also usually charge for inventory preparation, and for the final inspection. Inventories are essential. Sometimes these charges can seem very high, but inventories are a useful tool to both parties, and they do take some time to compile and check thoroughly. If you have a wide choice of property, the difference in agency fees can help you to decide which property to take. For tenants with very high rent levels, some negotiation may prove worthwhile. Whilst some agencies compile their own inventories, others sensibly use independent inventory services. Check on all these charges, and ask specifically if *any other charges* will be made by the agent either to set up, or to continue the tenancy. The last few charges need to be considered when working out what you can and cannot afford. Do also remember that agency fees for many other services can be very hefty. Not only do they levy high fees from the landlord for their services, but also their decorating, cleaning, and repair services can be very expensive.

Always remember when using any agency that it is the landlord who is their client – not you. Although many are helpful, they are employed *by* the landlord to work *for* the landlord. Some can be quite indifferent to the legitimate needs of the tenants, who do not in fact pay their fees. Do try to use an agency at least with staff who you feel comfortable with. You will, if your landlord uses an agent for management, need to deal with them every time you have an issue to resolve.

Sometimes properties available to let through agencies will be more expensive than similar properties available direct from private landlords. The landlord's agency fees have to be incorporated within the rent, and you will be paying them. Agencies usually charge landlords between ten to fifteen per cent plus VAT of the rent for management. For some tenants this is worthwhile, but others prefer to find their own landlord.

The private landlord

Check the local classified section or 'property to let' column. Many of the advertisements will have been placed by agents, but they are often required to indicate that they are trade (T), or to state their company. Some free advertising papers even require anything other than private advertising to be in bold print so that it is very easy to recognize.

Thousands of private landlords advertise here directly every day of the week. Check the price range you are looking for. Rental valuations depend on a number of different factors; the area, the condition, and the facilities offered. The valuations will vary, so check over a couple of weeks to get a feel for the price range you are looking for before you start making appointments to view. Take special care on locations, which can add or subtract huge sums to or from the rent. Know what you are looking for, and what you can afford, because you cannot afford careless mistakes.

When trying to work out what seems a reasonable rent, take into account what is being included. Many properties are offered part-furnished (P/F), which usually means carpets, curtains, cooker, fridge. Landlords and agents prefer it because there are strict requirements on the safety of supplied beds, sofas, etc. in fully furnished units, which will be detailed in a further chapter.

Naturally rental charges for fully furnished (F/F) can be a little higher. Do make sure you are comparing like with like.

If you take a fully furnished unit, and then want it unfurnished so that you can take your own furniture, it can actually cost you *more*, because you will have to pay for removal and storage of your landlord's belongings. Check the cost of this before you arrange it.

Properties which come fully furnished and equipped (F/F/eqpt.) have everything you should need (furniture, crockery, and sometimes even linen). The more you are being offered, the higher the rent. But don't try to economize on what you need. It isn't much of an economy to rent part-furnished and then have to spend a fortune buying furniture. After all, most tenants do not actually own a houseful of furniture. Never take a property which doesn't come complete with carpets, only the very rash would seriously consider carpeting a full house or flat on the basis of six months' guaranteed security.

Tenants taking fully furnished and equipped accommodation need not only an excellent inventory, they also need to live very carefully. One broken glass, which could have been part of a set of twelve, and full replacement of a complete new matching *set* could be required by the landlord or agent.

One final consideration is the manner in which you will pay the rent. If the property is advertised as a 'p.c.m.' (per calendar month) rent, you will make twelve monthly payments in any one year. If the rent is weekly, you will make fifty-two weekly payments in any one year. This can actually make quite a considerable difference – many landlords have thirteen months in their year!

Check it this way. If you are being quoted a weekly rent,

multiply it by fifty-two, and then divide it by twelve to check. The rent on what actually sounds cheaper, could in fact be quite a lot higher, and most experienced landlords and many long-standing agencies do not use p.c.m. rents for this very reason. Most agencies on the other hand do prefer them, because it makes their monthly accounting process easier.

Rent   £100 per week × 52   Total Annual Cost   £5200 per year
Rent   £400 pcm × 12   Total Annual Cost   £4800 per year

As this very clearly shows, there can be a difference of £400 per year between these rents due to the thirteenth month. Yet to the inexperienced, they sound broadly the same.

Prospective tenants are often advised to negotiate. This can be very much harder than your advisers might actually realize! Most landlords and agents will not even consider price negotiations, and in a market where good, or even decent property is at a premium, the reality is that your attempted negotiations may not be appreciated at all. Many landlords are actually quite uncomfortable about any nego-tiation. They may even take it personally, particularly if they feel that you are trying to 'knock down' a property they think is lovely! Try it by all means, but don't be espe-cially surprised if you're shown the door.

One genuine exception to this advice is for the cash-rich tenant (admittedly a bit of a rarity!). If you're in a position to pay your rent for several months in advance, this provides an excellent negotiating opportunity. Landlords who can't see the benefit in this arrangement are rarer than cash-rich tenants. For the rest of us, it is unfortunately a matter of looking around carefully for the best available unit, and paying, except in unusual circumstances, the rent asked for.

It can often seem much easier on balance to use an agency than to start ringing around the classifieds. Each tenant must balance convenience with cost. In addition you must decide whether or not you would prefer to know, and have direct access to, your own landlord, or whether you would be happier dealing through a third party. If you do intend to use any agency, try to find a recommended one, or one which is at least a member of one of their trading associations. If you decide to find property through the classifieds, you need to get a little organized before you pick up the phone. You need a pen and paper, and a list of sensible questions will save you time and disappointments (see below for suggestions). Any decent landlord will be more than happy to discuss these with you before you traipse miles for a viewing. It can be really frustrating trying to get information on the phone, but persevere. If the agency you call for details doesn't get around to sending the details they promised, ask yourself how reliable they are likely to be if the central heating breaks down in January. Find another agency. Similarly, if the private landlord you are trying to reach is permanently unavailable, or their partner doesn't know the answer to any of your questions, or the landlord simply cannot be bothered to chat to you on the phone for a few minutes, ask yourself the same question and again, find another landlord.

This author can absolutely guarantee that a conscientious landlord or agent will be responsive from the outset. If you are having difficulty communicating *before* you sign the contract, things are unlikely to improve once you have done so.

Sensible questions to ask before you make an appointment to view any property

How much is the rent, and is it payable weekly or monthly?
How much deposit is required, and how much rent is
    required in advance?

How is this to be paid – cash, cheque, banker's draft, building society cheque?

Are references/credit references required? How much will this cost?

What is included in the rent? Is there a washing machine? (include what you need)

How much are the water rates, and council tax?

How is the property heated?

Is there an inventory charge, and/or a vacating check charge?

What are you responsible for – gardens, decorating, etc?

What costs are shared with others in the building (e.g. electricity)?

Please note: if you do make an appointment to view, either keep it or cancel it. Don't just leave landlords standing outside a property waiting for you to turn up. It is unfair, discourteous and regrettably very common.

2 Viewings

After your deliberations, and your questions, you should by now have a list of several properties that you have made appointments to view. The advice given here is general, and you need to apply it to a wide variety of buildings. You should have appointments to view with either private landlords, or agency staff, and you still need to find out quite a lot. You are looking for a property that suits your needs, and is within your budget. Whilst to some readers of the guide, a price difference of a few pounds may be utterly immaterial, to other readers it can be absolutely critical. No matter how tight your budget though, you must find somewhere safe to live. At the bottom end of the market, this is not as easy as it ought to be.

Many properties, especially in this sector, are still technically unsafe, or unfit to live in. Although regulations exist to protect tenants, they are monitored by overburdened local authorities, who often do not even realize that a particular property is being rented out to tenants. There are a significant minority of landlords who operate quite outside the law, and who continue to offer dreadfully inadequate property to tenants. Included in this guide is a comprehensive list of all the legal duties a landlord should observe. These include basic maintenance of the property – however, simply reading the list doesn't really give a flavour of either the state nor the overall levels of dilapidation that some tenants see as they walk into a property to view.

Into this market come very many young people with very small budget. This chapter will try to give you some pointers on what to check for, whatever the price range.

Perhaps before we begin to consider the properties to be viewed, the very best advice you can take is never to view alone. There is simply too much to take in, and it is very difficult to remember everything, particularly if you're viewing more than one property. If you are looking to share with other tenants, you all need to view simultaneously. Landlords and agents can quite reasonably be reluctant to keep having to reshow one property to various members of a group. Additionally, it is simply not wise to make appointments to go into empty properties with anyone you have never met before.

> Sometimes, in an attempt to 'hold' a property, tenants agree to take it, hoping to find something that they prefer elsewhere. As soon as you have agreed in principle to accept a property, both landlords and agencies will want at least a proportion of the deposit, as a 'holding' deposit. This money will not be refunded if you later change your mind.

You would be quite amazed how many tenants are too embarrassed to say 'no thank you' to landlords and agents, and many would rather leave a small deposit than do so. If you definitely don't want it, say so. If you're undecided, say so. Never leave money thinking that you will get it back on request. Landlords and agents are quite used to hearing 'I'll let you know'.

If, however, you have paid part or all of the deposit and

do want the property, and the agency or landlord rejects *you* (say on referencing issues), you will be entitled to a refund of your deposit, but not in this instance the costs of referencing. If a private landlord or agent subsequently lets to someone else they prefer, again you will be entitled to a refund.

You may imagine that, having agreed to accept a property, no one else will have the opportunity to rent it. However, many landlords and agents do still continue viewings, usually because they have been let down themselves in the past. Similarly, most agencies will continue viewings until all the references you have provided are found to be acceptable. Do always remember that until all the necessary leases have been signed, and money exchanged, *no contract exists at all.*

If you really want a particular property, you need to ensure that the paperwork required by your agent or landlord is quickly made available, and that you have the money required ready and waiting. Do not expect anyone to hold a property for you for days or weeks while you sort yourself out. It simply won't happen.

How to start looking

If you are lucky enough to be able to visit the area and look at the properties from the outside before you have your viewing, so much the better. This is often an excellent way of screening out those properties you simply don't want before you go inside. However, if your viewing is the first opportunity you have to look at the property, look around carefully. Does it look horribly neglected? Is it in noticeably worse condition than its neighbours? Is the area worse than the flat you saw yesterday for the same rent?

If you are about to pay average or above average rent for the area, and the answer to these questions is yes, politely decline, and move on to your next appointment. However, if you are struggling to find something that you can afford, you probably have less choice. Unless horrified, continue your inspection.

Whether your budget is modest or generous, don't feel obliged to rush through this viewing in five minutes. If this were a second-hand car, you would want to check it over in a little detail. You might want some kind of mechanical report. It is a very common problem that landlords and agents try to hurry tenants. Always remember that they need tenants as much as you need a unit to rent. No one is running a charity here. This is a cold-blooded commercial transaction like any other, for a similar sum of money. You do not need hours to view, but don't allow yourself to be rushed through in a few minutes either. You, or your group, will be paying thousands of pounds to rent a property for a single year, and you will be contractually bound in most cases for at least six months. You are entitled to take a reasonable look. Don't feel pressured to make an instant decision. You can always go away and think about it for a short while.

What am I looking for?

Furnishings

Landlords and in some cases agents who let out property which is furnished are responsible under various laws to make sure that what they provide is safe. All upholstered furniture must comply with British Standards. This will usually mean that on beds, sofas, cushions, etc. you should find a triangular label with a BS trademark attached. More details on these are available in appendix 3, 'Basic Safety'. However, the easiest way of recognizing the symbol is to pop into any furniture showroom and have a look at a label. It is now illegal to sell furniture which doesn't comply with this requirement. If the label has been lost, the fabric label should be sewn into the item.

A very few landlords (who are not classified as investment landlords, for example those letting their own home for a relatively short time) are currently exempt from this requirement. However, the overwhelming majority of landlords and agencies are required to comply. If you know that this property is regularly let out, and that it isn't the landlord's own home, you know that this furniture should be in compliance. Don't take a property where the landlord is prepared to ignore this widely publicized rule. Who knows what else might not be safe? Responsible landlords don't provide dangerous furniture, and who wants an irresponsible landlord?

If the property is part-furnished it is simpler because there is less to check. Check that the carpets, curtains, etc. are in reasonable condition. Part-furnished properties should reasonably also have 'white goods', cooker, fridge, perhaps a dishwasher. Check that they work. Ask about service contracts, and, especially in more expensive units with a wide range of electrical goods, ask whom to contact if there is a problem, and how quickly repairs are usually made.

Unfurnished properties are perhaps the simplest of all – nothing to check for but doors, walls, windows, and a roof! Do check though that cooker points and plumbing for washing machines/dishwashers etc. are in place. You will also need a gas safety certificate for the gas boiler, if one is provided in the rent.

Some landlords are being approached by companies offering to 'spray' their old foam-filled non-compliant furniture to make it comply with British Standards! The landlord or agent may even show you a receipt to prove that this has been done. Anyone viewing property with furniture without BS labels, but with claims about 'treatment', should check with their local trading standards department for clear advice, and treat claims, for that is what they may well be, with some good-natured scepticism! If you're not convinced the furnishings are safe, look elsewhere. You might even feel confident enough to let the landlord know why you're not interested. If landlords often find their property rejected on safety grounds, they'll perhaps see the wisdom in complying with the law. We really cannot expect trading standards or environmental health officers to find every problem. Tenants too need to be proactive if standards are to be raised.

Gas appliances

Without any exceptions at all, every landlord or agent *must* make sure that *every* gas appliance has a current gas safety certificate. Lots of tenants are either too embarrassed, or too nervous of being shown the door to check for essential safety requirements. They shouldn't be, but in the real world tenants often feel quite intimidated, especially if they are inexperienced. No one is seriously suggesting that you carry out a full scale safety survey, but discreetly looking for labels on chairs is easy. If you are worried about asking for certificates, a more subtle approach can be applied. Casually ask how long it is since, say, the gas fire was serviced. Any responsible landlord or agent will be prompted to tell you about the annual safety check. If no information is volunteered, you really need to follow this up. Do you really want this flat enough to be slowly poisoned by carbon monoxide? Every landlord and some agents are liable to massive fines for ignoring this legislation. You seriously have to ask yourself – if your potential new landlord is willing to take this risk, what else is he prepared to risk that could be problematic? A few tips on what to look out for on badly maintained equipment are available in appendix 3, 'Basic Safety'. It is well worth the few minutes' reading before you go viewing.

This author recently heard the following tale from a student in the north of England. The gas fire in a student house did not work properly. Repeated calls to the landlord were ignored, and the tenants eventually called out a major gas company to look at the fire. The engineer declared the fire dangerous, but the tenants could not afford the repair. The engineer placed a sticker on the fire stating that the appliance was dangerous. It was May, and they managed without the fire. Weeks later, the landlord was showing around prospective tenants for the next academic year. He ripped off the sticker, and told the tenants that if they warned the new tenants, he wouldn't return their deposit!

Such conduct is hugely intimidating. If your landlord or agency doesn't make all the gas appliances safe, report them to the local Environmental Health Department of your local council.

Electricity supply

As well as the furniture being safe, and the gas appliances being regularly serviced and certificated, landlords are also expected to ensure that the electricity supply, and any electrical appliances, are safe. Unfortunately, this definition of 'safe' is rather more open, in a way that certification for gas appliances is not. Tenants must therefore exercise common sense. It is not being seriously suggested that you contact an electrician, but do look out for obvious problems as you do your viewing. Loose sockets, or too few, with numerous adaptors might concern you. Sockets in silly or unexpected places, such as really near the sink, or in a bathroom, might ring a warning bell. Single sockets can indicate an old-fashioned system. Round-pin sockets are definite ones to avoid.

Some landlords cover old wiring systems with shiny new switches and sockets. A brief look, say, in the cupboard under the stairs, can often readily reveal old rubber wiring. Here the value of taking someone else with you to view can really pay dividends. Whilst you innocently talk to the landlord about the lovely garden, your dad or your friend could be having a peek at the electrics under the stairs. If you're viewing with a reputable agency, no subterfuge is necessary. Ask when the last electrical check was carried out. They should have a note on file.

The author recently visited a student house in London. Old brown cloth covered wiring hung down to every light fitting. Many of the sockets were round pin. The landlord had augmented this admittedly deficient supply by stringing long lengths of wire from the lighting sockets to which numerous long block adaptors were attached. Admittedly, in a house with old furniture covered in brown nylon fabric, with suppurating bursts of foam guaranteed to suffocate in the event of a fire, one would not really have expected a recent wiring report. This landlord's only concession to modern standards was his realization that most of us don't have stereos with round-pin plugs these days.

Some other students were recently offered a flat with a washing machine *in the bathroom*, next to the bath. When challenged the agent insisted the bathroom was not a bathroom, but a washroom (which presumably just happened to have a bath and a toilet in it). Before you think that the washing machine might have been a welcome additional resource, just imagine the potential consequences of deciding to switch off the machine, whilst you were submerged in a deep relaxing bath!

Tenants really have to learn how to look out for their own safety. Most rented property is never even seen by a member of any authority.

General condition

Having looked at the features which may be obviously hazardous, you will also need to take in the general condition of the property. Do try to avoid, if financially feasible, properties in obvious stages of disrepair. Property ought to look fresh, clean and the contents in reasonable condition. This can be some of the most obvious evidence about the quality of the management. Neglected, unloved units will not change because you are moving in. Badly neglected property is owned or being run by someone who just doesn't care. This type of management is not usually very responsive if you genuinely need a repair, so try to find something better if you can.

However, sometimes appearances can be deceptive. It's amazing just what you can cover with a can of paint, and most people can be taken in by appearance occasionally.

Four tenants took a small, apparently pleasant terraced house during their second year at university. The bedrooms were freshly decorated, and everything looked fine. However, it soon became obvious that chronic damp was affecting one of the bedroom walls. The landlord did eventually arrange for works to be done. Unfortunately, the work judged necessary to sort out the damp plaster was to remove it all. The external repairs were never completed, the wall never replastered, and the tenant had little alternative but to sleep in a permanently damp room for two terms. To add final insult to injury, the landlord deducted the cost of redecoration . . . from the tenants' deposit . . . as there were some fingermarks on the wall!

Do try to help yourself as much as you can. The lettings industry is bedevilled with stories like this, and it is very hard for people who haven't been tenants to really believe what can and does go on. For most people, the upheaval of finding somewhere else, and getting a deposit returned in time to move on, can be so difficult that they have no choice but to accept bad housing. Tenants who have looked quite carefully do have at least a chance to pick up on some possible problems.

It can be awfully difficult when you come to vacate to prove that the chair was broken, or the carpets ripped *before* you signed the lease. Tips on all these matters can be found in the chapter on inventories.

Renting in groups

Some quite specific advice is needed for people who rent together in a group. Other information is required for tenants who, as individuals, rent a room, or a part of a house, which they share with others. This is a very complex area. Some further advice is available in Chapter 7, 'Leases', and Chapter 16, 'Houses in Multiple Occupation'.

If you fall into any of these categories some minimum additional safety standards may apply to you. If you are viewing a multi-occupied property, or a property which has been converted into flats or bedsits, you need to read the extra chapters. Generally you might expect to find fire doors (usually obvious, heavy doors with a self-closing spring or lever) or fire extinguishers. The law on this type of housing is highly complex, and unfortunately under constant challenge from landlords who are currently appealing against the safety standards which had been thought to apply. I'm delighted to say that the government is currently consulting to clarify the existing laws which govern safety in multi-occupied accommodation.

Try also to assess the arrangements in the property. Some landlords and agents are trying to multi-occupy properties in ways which can be difficult to live with. Four people, no matter how well they get on, living in a three-bedroomed house, with one of them occupying the only living-room, can cause problems because of lack of social space. Similarly three friends sharing the rent equally, whilst one has the master bedroom, and the other two have smaller ones, can cause real friction.

Sort out these issues *before* you sign the lease. There may be no alternative to this, but you ought to be aware in advance that it can be problematic. You are signing a legally binding contract, usually with a six-month 'fixed term'. This gives you your share of legal liabilities. You will not be able to walk away from it in three months if the mood takes you. In just the same way that your landlord cannot ask you to leave if he feels like a change (except within stringent legal requirements), you will also suffer significant financial penalties if you need to terminate early.

You also need to consider when sharing property, again before conflict arises, how shared bills will be met, as the following anecdote illustrates.

Four men sharing a four-bedroomed house ought not to sound problematic. However, in order to generate more rent, the landlord divided the accommodation oddly. Two tenants each had a bedroom plus a sitting-room with a gas fire, and two had only a bedroom. All shared the only kitchen and bathroom. Obviously, the two double-room lets were charged more rent. However, all were asked to share the bills equally. Clearly, the tenants with the cheaper accommodation were contributing more than their fair share, as they were paying towards their fellow tenants' sitting-rooms' running costs. This caused massive friction, yet each had signed contracts accepting this. Whenever a single room occupant vacated early, usually due to arguments, a new tenant accepted the same terms. Over the three years this arrangement ran, every time a tenant became frustrated by the unfairness of the arrangement and vacated early, the landlord refused to refund the deposit, and simply re-let.

Enquire before you accept any shared accommodation, especially in a multi-occupied house with fellow tenants who are unknown to you, how the bills are organized. Many well-run 'rooming houses', recognizing the problems, include all energy bills in the rent. If you are obliged to 'share' bills, be very wary. If you are to be individually charged, the best arrangement is for individual meters. Some landlords install individual gas or electricity meters for their tenants. However, there are legal limits on the profits which they can make on the resale of fuel to tenants. If you are at all concerned your local gas and electricity companies have booklets that help you ensure you are not being overcharged.

Where energy or water is included in the rent, your landlord must pay these bills. Sometimes tenants can find that they are threatened with disconnection because their landlord has not paid the account. In this instance, *immediately* contact your local council's private tenants officer or the Citizens' Advice Bureau for advice. They have powers to help.

3 Deposits

Whenever you decide to rent a property, you will be required to pay a deposit. This usually amounts to between four and six weeks' rent. A general rule of thumb is that more expensive properties with more expensive facilities will often charge toward the top end of the range, whereas four weeks (or one calendar month) is most common. Some properties require as much as the equivalent of two months' rent as a deposit. If you are asked to pay more than two months' rent, you really need to take some specialist advice. You may be able to claim that you have paid a 'premium', which confers some additional legal rights. Although unusual, sometimes less experienced landlords, having read or heard yet another horror story about a bad tenant, will try to cover their potential loss by holding more money. It is very unlikely to happen if you use an experienced landlord or agent.

Never (see previous chapter, 'Viewings') pay a holding deposit and then expect it back. They are almost invariably non-refundable, or at best partially refundable.

All landlords and agents need a deposit in order to safeguard the contents and condition of the property they are letting out. There is however no greater cause of dispute between parties than that of returns to tenants at lease end. Included in an appendix are two brief standard letters. The first is a letter requesting a deposit return, the second is a stronger letter for those who are experiencing some difficulty. This matter is so controversial that consumer associations have recently been urging the government to enact legislation on the Australian model, where all rental deposits are centrally held and administered. Millions of pounds are estimated to have been withheld annually from vacating tenants, some without question unfairly. The problems seem to be concentrated around a number of landlords and agents who consistently behave unscrupulously.

How deposits work

Having accepted a property one of two things will happen. You may initially be asked to provide a holding deposit, which is a sum less than the total deposit, but sufficient to cover the landlord's costs should you change your mind. Don't forget, the landlord has usually paid advertising costs and then may have turned away other callers because you have said you want to rent the property. For example, you might be asked for a hundred pounds to hold the property. This sum should then be *deducted* from the total amount of the deposit required at the later stage of handing over the balance of rent in advance plus deposit prior to moving in. If you are asked for 'key money', this is a separate additional charge. Avoid it wherever possible, it is a now quite unnecessary throwback to the days when the deposits held were only token sums. Alternatively, you may be required to pay the whole deposit as soon as you agree to accept the property. You should check this out when you ask your initial questions.

Do also check how this money needs to be provided. Some landlords require cash (but only usually for sums under about five hundred pounds. Some agents and landlords prefer cheques, banker's drafts or building society cheques. Ask what is required for your property, and when and how it needs to be paid. However a deposit is requested you must always insist on having a separate receipt for your deposit, and *keep it safe.*

Deposits belong to the tenant, not the landlord or agent. This sum of money is to be held by your landlord or agent as security, in case you damage, or allow to be damaged, any item or the building belonging to your landlord, or leave any unpaid bills behind when you leave. Many of the disputes which arise do so simply because people have either failed to understand what was expected of them, or chosen to ignore what was required of them. This applies to both landlords and tenants.

Deductions can be made if for example you make a cigarette burn in the carpet. Deductions cannot be made if a hole wears in the carpet, as this is 'reasonable wear and tear'. Routine redecoration cannot be charged for. However if you dirty, or mark, or damage in any way the decorations, you will be charged for the redecoration. If you decide to repaint the walls because you prefer a different colour, the landlord or agency can charge you for the cost of returning the property to its original colour, even if you think its an improvement. Electric kettles which wear out or break during normal use cannot be charged for. Ones that you have boiled dry and made the element melt can and will be.

Tenants really do have to come to terms with reading and *understanding* their leases thoroughly. If for example you move into a flat which is really scruffily decorated, do take care that your landlord hasn't inserted a 'tenants' responsibility for decorating' clause in your lease. If the garden looks like a wilderness, avoid an insertion in the lease to 'maintain' it. You're actually being obligated to improve your landlord's property, whilst paying them for the privilege!

Every time you decide to hang a picture, think carefully about your deposit. In some instances you can lose huge sums of money, especially in expensive properties where well-plastered walls have been damaged. Fitting a beautiful kitchen unit, or having a cable TV system installed, may seem like excellent ideas ... until you come to remove them when you leave. You will be charged for all damages you cause installing or fitting items. In some cases the items fitted can actually become the property of your landlord. Always remember, landlords exist to make a profit. They do not purport to be social workers, nor someone's long suffering parents. The arrangement into which you have entered is based on pure commerce, and your deposit can and *will* be utilized to pay the full commercial cost of any repairs necessary as a result of your conduct.

A young tenant recently wanted to put up a mirror in a lovely student house. Carefully, with a craft knife, he removed four small triangles of the wallpaper, drilled and plugged the wall, and hung his mirror. On leaving, he removed the mirror, opened a tobacco tin in which eighteen months previously he had carefully stored the four small triangles, removed the plugs, filled the holes, glued the triangles back in place, and left the flat. He received a full deposit return.

Do try to remember that story whenever you decide to do 'a little job' in any rented property. The contracts are tight, and you do need to be very careful. Nonetheless no landlord or agent has any right whatsoever to deduct any of your deposit without good cause. Familiarize yourself with both this chapter, and 'Inventories', and you should be better protected from some of their worst practices.

There is often a time lag, especially with agencies, between leaving and receiving any deposit return. This is quite reasonable. Do not panic if you have not received your money within a couple of days. Many landlords and agents like to check that all outstanding bills and accounts associated with your tenancy have been settled before they organize a refund statement. Further details are included on this, including how to help speed up the process, later on in the book. If you leave the property without having given proper notice, or before the end of the fixed term, your deposit will be always withheld to cover your rent (at least until your landlord has found a satisfactory replacement tenant).

Interest on your deposit

Many tenants do not realize that they are entitled to interest on their deposits. Your entitlement is at prevailing bank deposit rate, which you can find out through your own branch, or from your citizens' advisory services. Do make a claim for this money at the end of your tenancy. Just imagine how much interest the tenant deposits in a nationally based estate or lettings agents are generating every year if no one even asks for it back.

On some significant rents, especially in Central London, where deposit requirements can run into thousands of pounds, the interest alone could pay for professional cleaning services when you vacate. Each tenant needs to begin requesting this interest when they apply for their deposit returns. If you are subject to any deposit deductions, always check that the landlord or agent has taken your interest into account prior to doing their final calculations and returning your balance.

4   Inventories

The preceding chapter covered the payment of your deposit. In this section, we will be dealing with the contents and conditions which your deposit is designed to protect because, as was mentioned before, inventories and deposits are closely related.

Almost certainly you will be asked to agree and to sign an inventory, which will usually form the basis upon which your deposit return will, amongst other things be based. Your inventory is absolutely essential, and will, if managed properly, safeguard your own, as well as your landlord's interests.

Very occasionally, you will be offered a property without a written inventory, and where this does happen, it can be a very mixed blessing indeed. Without an inventory, *neither* party can actually prove what the original contents were, nor their original condition. Whilst at first glance you may feel happy about accepting a property without any inventory, remember that you are far more likely than the landlord to have to use the courts in the event of a dispute, and you will have no proof of the original condition. Whilst we don't suggest that tenants begin demanding inventories, you might sensibly be wondering why your landlord doesn't want to provide one.

Types of inventory

Let us however assume that an inventory has been produced, and consider its origins.

Independent inventories

Many expensive properties, and some average ones, are offered with the benefit of an independent inventory, usually compiled by a specialist company. This arrangement has the advantage of being (theoretically) much more impartial than other types, and the same company will usually complete a leaving check and assess if any damages or negligence (or home improvement!) have arisen. They will often also calculate the costs required to cover problems (often providing estimates), and advise the landlord or agency in writing of their findings. You should also be able to obtain a copy of both reports.

This is a highly satisfactory arrangement, and whilst it can seem expensive (the costs are often shared between landlord and tenant), it has the undoubted advantage of independence. Any tenant renting property with a relatively high rent is strongly urged to consider the advantages of this type of service.

Tenants in high-rent areas, even where they have already been charged by their agent or landlord for alternative 'in-house' services, should very seriously consider the advantages of paying for their own independent assessment at lease beginning and end. In Central London for example, some rents are thousands of pounds per month, and this is a sensible safeguard for what will be a significant deposit.

'In-house' inventories

More usual are agencies whose own staff draw up the inventory, and conduct the final inspection. A note of caution here is that many agencies also run a number of smaller companies/operations within the overall service offered to landlords, e.g. cleaning companies, or decorating or gardening services. A sceptical person might consider the advantages therefore in finding problems with the condition of the property once you have vacated. This is a highly lucrative sideline for many operators, and there is no independent scrutiny of agencies, nor are there any qualifications required before you can set one up. If you have left the property as you accepted it, you should expect your money back. Use the letters in the appendix and challenge any unreasonably high, or unfair charges. Further advice on this is given in the chapter 'When the Tenant Decides to Leave'.

Privately compiled inventories

Compiled by private landlords, these inventories can be either highly professional, thorough documents, or a brief, handwritten note. The same warning about objectivity applied to 'in-house' inventories should also be applied here. They may be free, or chargeable. You need to enquire.

What to check

However formal or informal, these inventories are meant to represent the contents of the property, and their condition. In some instances they also state the decorative condition of the premises you are about to rent. You need to check any inventory very carefully. Too often, embarrassed tenants simply smile at the landlord, and say they're sure it's OK. This has happened to me many times. I always insist that tenants both read and check the inventory because it is our *mutual* protection.

Draw any deficiencies to the attention of the landlord or agent. If you are asked to sign an inventory in an agency office having previously visited the property, ask to revisit beforehand to check the property. It is vitally important. If you find for example that the inventory simply says 'sofa' but you can see a couple of cigarette burns or it looks slightly soiled, ask politely for this to be noted on the inventory. If you meet with a refusal to change the inventory, start asking yourself why. This process can actually take a little time. Some landlords and agents can look rather pained if you want to be thorough. Ignore the rather pointed clearing of throats and glancing at watches that can accompany this process, and don't just sign anything to get hold of the property. Obvious deficiencies can truly come back to haunt you in this business.

Having read and agreed the contents of your inventory, you will be expected to sign it as a true reflection of the property at the time you took possession of it. You must always ask for your own copy and keep it safe. This really isn't something you should throw in with a variety of other bits and pieces. As emphasized before, these are important, legally binding documents which need careful storage.

Safeguarding your deposit

This all sounds so easy, doesn't it? Ask to visit the property, take the inventory, have all the time you want to examine it, ask for anything that concerns you to be included on it before you sign, and bingo, you're all set!

The reality can sometimes be a little different, as every relatively experienced tenant reading this will know. This particularly applies at the lower end of the price range, where there are some fairly unsavoury characters involved in letting property.

You may be renting a property with stains too numerous

to mention on the furniture. You may be struggling to find something which you can afford, and the agent is telling you that he has eight other people interested! You may very well on this type of property *never even see* a written inventory.

Because property in certain price ranges is in very high demand the last thing you can afford to seem is 'picky'. The truth is the last thing some landlords and agents really need is a tenant trying to look after their own interests. You may not get the property at all. This may not sound too bad, if the property is in dubious condition, but in truth you may have very few alternatives. Sometimes tenants find that they have little alternative but to take a property that they know is less than ideal. In these circumstances, a slightly different approach may be required. If you are going to accept the property irrespective of the condition, you still need quietly to protect your interests. Even a modest house, or flat in most cities, will be holding a deposit of hundreds of pounds, and you need to be able to get it back! It is too often forgotten that for some of us, at certain times in our lives, the loss of even a hundred pounds can cause a great deal of hardship. It should also be remembered that most tenants have to plan and save for, or even borrow, the deposits on their homes. The unfair loss of even a proportion of it can trap people in poor homes, because their deposit return is needed to fund their new deposit. This can be oppressive, and tenants in these circumstances need to act thoroughly to secure their own interests. You may have to sign an inventory which simply gives a list of items, with no indication of their condition. It may state 'all items in good clean condition', when they are not.

Here are a few practical tips which can genuinely help. Take someone with you, preferably *not* a relative or a close friend, who can give independent evidence should you need it about how things really were when you moved in. Take a photocopy of the inventory you have signed and, on the first day of your tenancy, note every problem on your inventory and post it registered post to your landlord or agent. Ask the tenant next door to pop in and see what things are like before you unpack your things (although they are only likely to agree if it is unlikely to aggravate their landlord). A neighbour who isn't the landlord's tenant and who isn't concerned may be prepared to help.

The following is a procedure that is worth following if you do not have the security of an independent inventory.

- On the day that you take possession, as your first task, go through the whole property thoroughly, either with your inventory which you have signed, or making your own.
- Make a careful note of everything in the property, and make a particular note of everything which is damaged, marked or broken.
- If mould is evident, make a note of its position and extent. It is horribly common in rented property and can ruin your belongings as it is impossible to wash out.
- Make a detailed list of everything which concerns you, e.g.: cooker rings that are loose or do not work, stains on beds, coffee-ring stains on tables, loose sockets, etc.
- Detail the stage of the decorations, including whether or not they are in good condition.
- If possible, take photos of any damaged items, putting that day's newspaper headline and date clearly and visibly in the picture. Place the newspaper as close to the damaged item as possible.
- Have your photographs developed immediately, a same-day service is best.
- Place your detailed list plus your photographs in an

envelope as soon as possible, and mail them registered post to yourself at your new address.

- When the envelope is delivered put it somewhere very safe, but on no account open it.

If there is any dispute when you come to leave the property about the condition it was in when you took possession, you can simply tell the landlord or agent that you took the precaution of obtaining proof. Do not at any stage either give them the envelope or break the seal, but explain what steps you took to protect your deposit. This will be valuable evidence if you need to go to court over any dispute, and landlords and agents will recognize this very quickly! What's more, the total cost is only about five pounds, which isn't much for the protection.

If this all seems a trifle over the top, just remember that it is estimated that every year millions of pounds is unlawfully deducted from tenants' deposits by unscrupulous landlords and agents. It is amazing to me that tenants don't take more steps to protect themselves. I can't imagine any other circumstances where intelligent people would hand over hundreds of pounds to someone that they have only known for a matter of minutes, trusting the integrity of the stranger on the basis of a handwritten receipt.

As tenants you do not need to be confrontational, but you should try to be proactive. By reading this and spending a few minutes once every six months or a year when you move, you could yourself ensure that you are not willingly contributing a few hundred pounds annually to this staggering sum of 'lost' funds.

Do always remember that those landlords and agents engaging in sharp practice are relying on your lack of knowledge, or planning. They cannot exploit well-prepared tenants. Unfair deductions tend to rely on your ignorance.

The less of it you show, the less likely you are to experience problems.

5   Other Requirements

As well as leases, inventories, and deposits, a whole range of other requirements can be made of new tenants. The only important thing you need to remember is that everything you sign can become a part of your contract, and you can be held to it!

From tenants

Tenant application forms

These are fast becoming adopted by many landlords and agents. Since 1997, one of the grounds upon which tenants can be asked to leave (even during the relatively safe fixed period), is ground 17, and the period of notice of your landlord's intention to seek possession in this case can be as little as two weeks (see Chapter 15 for further details on grounds for possession).

   Ground 17 allows landlords to act if they were persuaded or induced to grant the tenancy as a result of a false statement, knowingly made by the tenant, or someone acting at the tenant's instigation. This was a very significant addition to the rights of possession your landlord had before 1997, and a necessary one. Tenants who now claim to be employed when they are not, for example, could be affected. So too could tenants who pretend to be older than they in fact are, where landlords have age restrictions. Students have often failed to admit that they are students because many landlords do indeed avoid them. Application forms are a protection for landlords and agents against any such false statement.

This ground enables landlords who have been told untruths to use that as a legal reason for the return of their property. Tenancy application forms are a useful way therefore of making sure that landlords and agencies have written proof of the tenants' claims. Prospective tenants would be well advised to remember this when filling them in.

Parental guarantor forms

It is a common requirement that the under-21s (sometimes up to under-25s) are asked to have a parent or guardian guarantee the landlord that they will make good damage or unpaid rent. When one sees the utter devastation that can be wreaked on a perfectly good house in a matter of days by a tiny minority of tenants, the reason for this becomes clear.

A responsible landlord, having just refurbished a whole house, rented it at 8 p.m. to three young people. When he returned the next morning, as arranged, to do one final job in the new kitchen, he found that the contents of the coffee machine had been tipped into the centre of the new lounge carpet, and five cigarette ends had been stubbed out and left in the centre of the coffee. They had been in place less than twelve hours and had caused over four hundred pounds worth of damage!

In order to protect themselves from such behaviour, many in the industry now insist that they have real come-back on a parent for example. These documents are often drawn up by a solicitor, and are legally binding. Having read the story above, you might understand why they are sometimes asked for. If you are not convinced read on.

A young, unemployed man took a flat. His mother clearly wanted him to leave home, and paid the deposit; she also happily signed a parental guarantor form for the agent. Her son moved in, and within a week, the two tenants downstairs contacted the agent. Hot water was pouring through their bedroom ceiling. An emergency plumber was sent to investigate. The tenant had acquired an automatic washing-machine, and had fitted it himself. The plumber looked, and asked where the waste-pipe had been fitted. 'What waste-pipe?' Perhaps the one still fitted snugly with plastic ties to the base of the machine. Gallons of hot soapy water had run through the building that week.

The agent decided to visit and have firm words with the tenant. When the lad opened the door, a big-footed Rottweiler puppy jumped up to greet him. Another impulse purchase? When contacted the mother simply had no idea of the implication of the document she had so recently signed, and would be held to by a rightly efficient agent. 'But surely you can claim on the insur-ance?' was her response. A full repair account was sent to the mother.

Tenants need to understand that they or their guarantors will be held liable for their own conduct. All the documen-tation you are asked to sign has a purpose.

Other types of guarantee

Sometimes tenants have circumstances which require specialist guarantees. An excellent example of this is for the tenant who wants to move in, say, with the family dog. Most leases specifically exclude pets, but if you need a home with your dog, and you discuss it in advance, many agents and landlords will agree. They do however normally expect you to provide additional levels of deposit against damage, perhaps the equivalent of two months' rent, and often ask you to sign a guarantee that you will replace to their satisfaction any items (including garden lawns) that have been damaged. They also usually demand additional end-of-lease cleaning.

From landlords and agents

When exchanging various documents with your landlord, you can also ask for copies of the following which you might find useful:

- Service contracts, if they apply to equipment in the property you are renting.
- Gas safety certificates, if you haven't already been shown them.
- Certificates of insurance, particularly public liability insurance, which all landlords should have.

Most landlords restrict their insurance to their own building and contents. For most tenants, arranging insurance cover for their own things is an additional cost. If you cannot do so easily, try a broker. If all else fails and your family agree, it is often possible to have your parents

extend their own household policy to cover your possessions in the event of a loss. If you are in full-time education
your student union will help you to arrange it easily.

6 Living as a Tenant

So many areas of dispute between landlords and tenants arise because of simple misunderstandings. Both landlords and tenants are often genuinely unsure about their areas of responsibility. This section is designed to help you understand your status as a tenant better, by explaining in simple terms what you can expect from your landlord, and what he/she can expect from you.

Living as a tenant is quite different from, say, living at home. It is also very different from living in any property as an owner-occupier. You have a formal contract which governs your behaviour and the manner in which you live, and you really do have to abide by it if you want your tenancy to be trouble-free. Here there's no one else to clean up after you, and you will be charged if you leave a mess behind when you leave. In this arrangement, no one will good-humouredly accept a broken chair-leg, or a burn mark from the iron on the dining-room table. Whatever damage is caused by you, however small, you will be billed the full commercial rate for its repair. The cost of these repairs can be very surprising, especially to those of us with 'handy' parents.

You are not free to redecorate without consent, and if you do need consent for anything, especially if you are dealing with an agency, you need it in writing. Landlords and agents are often in major dispute behind the scenes about how many deductions are to be made from your deposit. Agencies can find that whilst they may judge that a full deposit return is due, the landlord is demanding deductions. As stated before, agents are employed by landlords, not tenants. Many agents have given a written undertaking to their landlords that they will not release deposit refunds without the landlord's consent. If you have only your word that the agency said it was OK to redecorate, there may be problems when you leave.

Let us start with simple things first. If you break anything, you will need to pay for its replacement. You may alternatively be asked to replace it yourself. Do make sure that you are replacing like with like. Do not replace a beautiful mirror with a cheap alternative, or a couple of mirror tiles. It will not be accepted on final inspection. Conversely, dispute demands for a beautiful mirror, if the one you broke was a mottled old thing. It is also best not to throw away the broken bits of anything away, until you are sure that your landlord or agent is satisfied with the replacement you are suggesting, because you will have a terrible problem proving the likely value of anything you tossed in the bin!

The basic requirement of your lease is that you return the property to the landlord in the same condition as when you moved in. With a broken item, it is relatively easy to sort out. Things can get a bit more complicated when responsibility is a little blurred. If for example the main drain blocks, and sewerage is seeping odiously around the back door, the landlord or agent need to be informed so that they can initiate repairs. If it is a problem with the condition of the drains, that is the landlord's responsibility. If however you have blocked the pipe by stuffing disposable nappies down it all week, the cost of unblocking and clean-up will be yours, even if the land-lord or agent insists on making all the necessary arrangements.

Never assume that your landlord's insurance will cover your own negligence. Many insurers will pay out to the landlord, and then seek to recover their costs from the responsible party. It is no good therefore setting the chip pan alight, and expecting someone else to pay for your own carelessness.

As a tenant, you are also liable for the conduct of anyone else you invite into your landlord's property. Damage during parties is a classic example. If there is damage caused, the costs will be down to you. Additionally, you are expected to behave 'in a tenant-like manner', and you must take sensible precautions against damage. Some landlords may ask you to sign an additional list of terms, or may have a very comprehensive lease drawn up with specific requirements and responsibilities for their tenants. These might include things like 'to play music, TV, etc., with due consideration for other residents', or 'to leave heating on during any winter periods when the tenant is absent from the building for more than twenty-four hours'. If you can't satisfy the terms, don't sign it. Never sign and then assume that ignoring terms will work. It won't.

An apparently responsible tenant left his rented house in Macclesfield to visit his parents in Hampshire, and, in an attempt to economize, turned off the central heating boiler and went home for ten days. A severe cold snap burst the water mains supply-pipe in the roof. Over the next several days, tens of thousands of gallons of water coursed through the empty building, drawing the attention of the neighbours only when a glassy puddle decorated the front steps. By the time the management was called, every ceiling in the building was down, and not one item of contents salvageable. Both landlord and tenant lost everything they owned. The landlord was insured, the tenant had economized on insurance. The tenant needed rehousing for two months until the property had been repaired. Unsurprisingly, he was not offered an extension to his fixed term.

There are some circumstances in which the condition of the building adversely affects the tenants. Lots of cheaper housing has a condensation problem, and condensation is a major cause of mould. This can grow on one's clothes, which are ruined, and destroy your personal possessions. This problem is one which is usually the responsibility of the landlord. In these circumstances tenants can act against the landlord, if they are willing to do so. Damp and mould are associated with ill health, and some tenants have successfully, with the help of legal advisors, sued landlords. If only possessions are affected, write to your landlord, with a list of damaged goods, and if all else fails, sue for their replacement through the small claims court, even after your tenancy has ended if they did not respond to your letters whilst you lived there.

Even in prestigious properties things can go awry. Here, lavish features or fittings included in the rent must work, and continue to work if they are included in the rent. If repairs are slow, hustle. Believe me, if your rent is slow you will be hustled!

The tenant of a luxury property reported to their agent that the expensive dining-room table-leg was wearing loose. The agent promptly reported this to their client the landlord, who did not get around to authorizing the agent to have the table-leg repaired. Subsequently the tenant was entertaining some colleagues at a lavish dinner party when the leg finally gave way, demolishing his party and his personal china. This tenant took his landlord to court for the loss.

Can the landlord visit the property whilst I am a tenant?

Landlords do have a statutory right (under the 1988 Act) to enter the property at reasonable times of the day to carry out repairs, or to inspect the condition of their property. Extra additional rights of entry are sometimes included by landlords in leases. However, they should give you twenty-four hours' notice in writing. Some landlords also reserve immediate rights of entry for emergencies. However, these landlords' rights of entry don't allow them to come and go as they please. Landlords need to ask permission to enter, hence the need for twenty-four hours' notice. As a tenant you are buying with your rent the right of 'quiet enjoyment'. The property you are renting is your home, and good landlords and agents will automatically respect this.

Two charming tenants moved out of a lovely property that they were renting because, being polite, and as usually tenants are somewhat deferential towards their landlady, they could not stop her from coming into the property each day and tidying up! She lived in the same road, and each morning as she passed she needed to call in, usually because the tenants 'hadn't got the curtains right'.

This was in all other respects an excellent landlady, offering an excellent quality of unit. Unfortunately she simply had no idea how anyone could refuse her the right to go into her own property. The fact that other people were paying her money to live there did nothing to discourage her from the view that it was still 'hers'.

Some tenants however find that they are living in property that is simultaneously up for sale. In these instances tenants are entitled to the same notice of intention to inspect as in any other circumstances, unless something other has been specifically inserted into the terms of the contract. Estate agents are still bound to offer tenants in buildings they are trying to sell a right of 'quiet enjoyment'.

Some of the most useful advice that this author can give about problem solving during tenancies, is to develop the best working relationship you can with your landlord or agent. This industry is bedevilled by the conflicting histories of Rachman versus the Tenant from Hell, and if you're too young to know who Rachman was, he's now in the Oxford Dictionary, look him up! Don't forget that, all too often, either landlord or a tenant have had previous problems which prejudice their views of each other. The landlord who seems to have rule after rule may have had a previous very bad experience. There are awful tenants as well as awful landlords. Remember that, in the future, when you need to rent again, there is nothing more useful than a glowing reference from your previous landlord. Landlords do see their fair share of irresponsible behaviour, and can get very frustrated dealing with the irresponsible behaviour of this tiny minority.

A landlord, looking for a small set of drawers for a flat, called by a second-hand dealer he knew. Seeing a small chest he liked, he noticed other items which also looked good . . . and rather familiar. Closer inspection revealed the entire contents of one of his own properties on display. Everything was there, from the carpets to the lightshades. Before moving out, the tenant had sold the entire contents of his landlord's flat to a dealer for a small sum of money. Landlords as well as tenants, do have their problems.

So wherever possible try for good terms with whoever is managing your property. Tenants renting property through agents can, in many ways, have a quite different set of problems to tenants dealing directly with their own landlord. Agencies act as 'brokers' between landlords and tenants, drawing money for their role as go-between. Although this sometimes works well, too often tenants find it is used as an excuse for failure to manage the property well. 'We still haven't heard back from the landlord' is not much consolation if you're waiting for an essential repair. It can however work equally badly for the unsuspecting landlord sometimes.

A tenant took a pleasant property, with no apparent problems. A couple of days later he called the agency, complaining about slugs in the kitchen. Billing the landlord by the hour, the agency sent out a maintenance man, who found one slug trail on the doormat. He inspected, and reported back. Numerous phone calls and much abuse followed, the agents responding with *seven* call-outs, and the laying of slug pellets, traps and salt, and billed by the hour to the unsuspecting landlord. Apparently one particularly resolute slug had decided that this was going to be his nocturnal route whatever anyone else thought! In this case, the unreasonable demands of the tenant rather than the landlord resulted in a large deduction from the landlord's revenue.

Being a tenant doesn't absolve you from all normal domestic tasks. As famously said by Lord Denning, 'the tenant must take proper care of the premises . . . he must do the little jobs around the house which a reasonable tenant would do'.

Subletting

Most assured shorthold leases specifically exclude subletting. This is considered as quite a serious breach of terms by most landlords. If you want a partner to move in, most landlords or agents will not object, so long as the partner's name is put on the lease.

Rental payments

You must pay your rent on time, and in the manner agreed with your landlord. Landlords and agents are running businesses and the sole reason that you occupy their properties is for the income that you generate. Excuses, late payments, and insufficient payments are simply unacceptable.

There will in some instances be a genuine reason, as opposed to an excuse, why your rent will not be available. Get on the phone and discuss this immediately with whoever manages your property. It is most unwise just to not say anything, to go out when the collection is due, or just to not pay. Nor do you enjoy the right (except in some serious and rare cases for which you would need legal advice before you tried it) to withhold payments because, in your opinion, the landlord or agent haven't fulfilled their obligations. The matters are separate, and need to be dealt with in almost all cases separately.

A ground for your landlord to use for possession is that you have been persistently late paying your rent. Proof of current arrears is not always required. The payment record can be considered. If you pay your rent weekly you are legally entitled to a rent book. If you pay by cash, ask for and save all receipts as proof of payment. Always ask when your tenancy is starting and, if the rent is to be collected, by whom. You do need to be certain that you don't pay one person, not get a receipt, and then find that a further person calls for the money. Before you imagine this can't happen, let me assure you that it can. Student tenants in

Birmingham last year paid one of the brothers in a family their rent (in cash . . . no receipt), only to find the brother whom they normally paid arrived an hour later for the rent! It can sometimes be quite difficult to placate an aggressive landlord, and they do exist.

7 Leases

Almost every tenancy now available to you will be one type or another of assured shorthold tenancy. This chapter gives very general advice on leases. For more specific information, see Chapters 10 and 11.

Leases are very important legal documents. They must be signed by both landlord and tenant (or agent). They must be witnessed to be valid. In addition they should also be stamped by the Inland Revenue, for which a tiny fee (fifty pence at time of writing) will need to be paid by the tenant. Don't therefore be surprised if your landlord asks you for your newly signed lease, because he needs to send both signed copies along for stamping. Don't even be surprised if no one ever mentions it. Many landlords and even some agents don't bother doing it, although in theory the lease is invalid for court proceedings until this process has been completed.

You are legally obliged to observe all the terms of the lease you have signed, unless something has been added which is not within the legal framework of the Act. The most common is for a landlord to try to extend the month's notice required from the tenant. Any unreasonable additions to terms, or things that conflict with the law, will automatically be overridden by the legislation. If you are seriously concerned by something in your lease, contact the local authority or CAB for a little advice.

Break clauses

Sometimes, before agreeing to rent a property for a fixed period of time, a tenant will ask for a 'break clause' to be inserted. These give an opportunity for a tenant to leave on a certain date, agreed mutually before the tenancy begins. They are not standard clauses, and will certainly not be found in a standard lease. They are quite common in more expensive units, and almost standard in company lettings. Your average landlord will almost certainly not be interested in paying to have one inserted into their leases. Seek specialist advice, or use a reputable agency if you are looking for this type of arrangement.

Joint tenancies

Where one tenant rents one unit they will accept full responsibility for the tenancy. Where two people, e.g. two partners, sign a lease, this is a joint tenancy. Joint tenancies can also be used for small groups of sharers. In a joint tenancy, every tenant who signs the one lease is bound by the same terms.

In a group of tenants this can be significant. If one tenant decides to leave, and gives notice to the landlord/agent, technically the tenancy of you all can fold. Alternatively, if one tenant leaves, and the others with their landlord agree to stay on, the remaining tenants are responsible for the whole of the rent, not just the percentage they were paying before. These tenancies carry what is known as 'joint and several liability'. These tenancies are complex, as are a number of other ways of occupying houses either as groups, or collections of individuals. A more detailed breakdown of some of these, is available in the chapter on 'Houses in Multiple Occupation'.

Joint tenancies are quite complicated to run. It can be really difficult for example when one tenant wants to leave, *and* wants their share of the deposit back. The landlord or agent won't give back any part of the deposit before the property has been vacated and inspected. In some cases they *will* let you find another sharer, and the new tenant can 'buy out' the outgoing tenant's share of the deposit by paying them direct. If you are the new tenant, make sure the landlord or agent has your name on the lease, or the deposit return can go to the person you've just paid off!

You may be offered a whole new lease, or a replacement may be offered with the same dates but different names. If one party doesn't pay their share of the rent on time, the rest of you will have to make it up. If one party causes major damage, you are all jointly responsible for the total cost. Many a large deposit has evaporated in this way. These tenancies can be messy, and fraught with unseen problems. You need to thrash out all these types of problems *before* you embark on one.

The alternative, of each separate tenant having a separate lease, can cause landlords to find themselves in very difficult circumstances. If four people share on individual leases, and one gives notice to quit, whilst the other three wish to remain, the landlord faces either a period of three-quarters rent only being paid, or the unenviable task of trying to find another single person to 'fit in' with the existing tenants. The landlord may also face the impossible task of trying to assess who is responsible for damage or mess, as one tenant demands a deposit return, and all the others deny responsibility for damage.

Simply because combining a number of tenants in one property can be so complicated, agents and landlords will usually only accept them on joint leases. Basically this appears currently to allow landlords and agents to also combine a number of people into one 'household', all signing the same lease on the same terms. These houses then appear to often fall outside the safety requirements for houses in multiple occupation.

The criteria for what *in law* makes a 'house in multiple occupation' is currently under challenge through the courts, by landlords seeking to avoid complying with the existing safety regulations for these types of property (see Chapter 16 for further information). I frequently hear cases where environmental health departments try to take action against this type of housing, and get little support from the tenants, who seem quite happy to accept accommodation if it is convenient. This is a bit like being happy to drive a car with bad brakes. Everything's fine till you need them!

Young people particularly have always rented collectively for economy. As rents soar and contracts tighten, this particular group is one of the most vulnerable. Students are especially hard hit by these problems.

Where a number of individuals share one property, it may be considered a house in multiple occupation (HMO). Landlords and agents are then responsible for making sure that adequate safety standards are in place. Some of the reasons why this is important are obvious. If a number of people are coming and going, leading relatively independent lives, who knows who's in and who's out if there's a fire? If individual tenants are trying to maintain a private space, bedroom doors often have locks which can cause problems with escape in emergencies which wouldn't normally apply in a family unit. With five individuals cooking, fire risk is increased, and so on.

In the recent past, if you were living with several others on a joint tenancy, the environmental health department of your local council could, if they thought the arrangements unsafe, serve a notice on your landlord or agent, legally obliging them to carry out basic safety measures. The regulations for HMOs were thought to apply to some student houses also, but a recent legal case, *Sheffield* v. *Barnes*, has thrown this already controversial area into considerable confusion. Until this case (1996), these regulations were thought to apply to some student housing. The Sheffield case has cast doubt on whether this is the case. Up and down the country landlords and agents are using this case as a precedent, and challenging many notices, in many differing types of case.

The government is currently trying to work out legislation to clarify this major problem, and is considering the licensing of all landlords offering specific types of accommodation. Many councils have also introduced legally enforceable registration of landlords, so standards can be enforced.

It is, however, a depressing situation that, at the moment, until such legislation is finally worked out, we appear to be going backwards in terms of safety. More depressing still that some of the youngest, or relatively impoverished tenants clubbing together for economic necessity, find themselves at the cutting edge of attempts to reduce even the most basic requirements of safety.

Why your lease length matters

Tenants, no matter how well informed they are, can still find themselves in property which is unfit to live in, or unsafe. The huge demand, particularly in university towns, has caused a real shortage of affordable accommodation of reasonable quality. If you have been able to obtain a lease from your landlord or agent which covers the full period you wish to live there under the 'fixed term', you do have the relatively safe option of asking your local environmental health department to inspect, and at least check if you are covered under existing laws. They may still be able to take some action to force your management to improve safety standards.

If however you have only been able to obtain a 'fix' of six

months when perhaps you need nine, or you have a year's short-term employment contract, you run the genuine risk of not being able to stay on beyond the original fixed term. Landlords running unsafe multi-let properties can take a very dim view of being 'reported to the council'.

The security that negotiating a lease for the length of time you are likely to need becomes obvious now. Tenants dependent on lease extensions are often too afraid to complain about anything at all. It can take a brave person indeed to insist to some of the more assertive landlords that, as tenants, they enjoy certain rights, however limited. Being prepared before you become a tenant is the best safeguard you can have; being aware if you already are a tenant is the second best. Never forget, your lease does offer you some valuable safeguards, if you know where to look for them. Whilst landlords may become a little belligerent, they too are bound by the lease that they have signed.

Licences

Some landlords (or licensers) run properties with a number of rooms let on an individual basis. Whilst many are genuine licences, others are in fact and in law tenancies (see also Chapter 10).

Licences are usually offered to restrict your security of tenure. Whilst it is perfectly possible, and in some instances appropriate, to offer them, quite strict rules apply to what is and what isn't genuine. Landlords using licences often do so in large properties, and licensees don't enjoy any luxuries such as 'fixed terms'. They are all too often shorthand for 'if you don't like it, leave'.

In the past, 'licensees' who have been asked to leave have taken legal advice, and found that they never had a licence, their landlord had created a tenancy by mistake, often with considerable unknown rights. Many of these are outlined in the following chapters, however, it is worth repeating that it is genuinely very difficult for any person who does not actually live in the building (or member of their family) in which you have been given a licence to issue a licence. If your landlord doesn't live on the premises, or owns a number of buildings filled with occupants, as is common, she or he will very often have offered a licence, but may easily have inadvertently granted a tenancy. This may be a genuine lack of knowledge on their part, or a deliberate attempt to reduce your rights. If you have exclusive use of any part of any property, your own room for example, that no one else enters; or if you have been given any specific length of time which you can occupy the building; you are very much more likely to have a tenancy than a licence.

Anyone reading this guide who has been told the agreement is a licence, or has a written licence, is advised to read Chapter 10 with particular care. It may even be that when you came to view the room the 'landlord' said something along the lines of, 'Oh, I don't bother with all that stuff. Everyone here gets along fine. No need to make anything too official. If people aren't happy, they just move on.' It's like buying a car without a log book. Be a little suspicious. If you still want to take it, because you like it, or because it's cheap, take it by all means. But once you are settled, quietly find out where you stand legally.

Lodgings

Genuine lodgings, where you live as part of someone's home, offer very little security of tenure. Naturally it is only right that someone offering accommodation as part of their own family unit has the option to ask a lodger to leave if they don't fit in. Lodgers also are usually able to leave very easily for exactly the same reasons. They are a very old-fashioned, and often excellent, alternative to living in a lonely house with few facilities, and few comforts. There are striking successes and striking failures, but effectively they offer no security of tenure.

Sensible advice on leases

There is still a widely held perception in this country that tenants have somehow failed the financial test of being home owners. This is absolute nonsense. For many of us it is the most financially astute decision, and it is often far more expensive in the short term than paying a mortgage. If you are signing a lease on any property here are some sensible tips.

- Read it – you would be amazed how few people do – and preferably before you sign it!
- Work out how long you will need to live in the property, and try to negotiate the longest convenient lease length you can. Always try to maximize the fixed term if you are certain you want to live there for a certain length of time.
- If you don't think you want to stay long, try to negotiate the shortest fixed term available. If all else fails, try for a break clause. If you only need to rent for three months, try not to take a lease for six; the likelihood is that you will end up paying through the nose for the privilege.
- If you are being asked to sign a licence agreement, get it checked out at some time. You may have accidentally just been offered a tenancy.
- Don't sign anything that worries you. Unreasonable clauses need to be deleted, not agreed to and optimistically ignored.
- Observe all the clauses in the lease you agreed to sign, not just those you like.
- Keep all your documentation safe.

8 When You Decide to Leave

When you decide that the time has come to move on, or your fixed term is nearing completion, you need to organize yourself all over again. It isn't a strict legal requirement in all cases, but it is always a good idea to write to your landlord or agent to confirm that you will be leaving, and you should always do this at least a month before your chosen leaving date. Date the letter, and give the exact leaving date in the letter. For some types of assured shorthold this is a legal requirement, for others it may not be. It is always a good idea to err on the side of caution. If you were legally obliged, perhaps hidden within some other piece of paperwork you signed, and you fail to provide formal notice, you may face weeks of hassle trying to get a deposit refund. It is so unnecessary, when a few words in the post will ensure that you have covered yourself.

Even for those who have a clearly stated fixed term, confirmation in writing is still highly advisable. Many tenancies which started out as six-month leases run on and on as statutory periodics when all parties are quite happy. Initial short fixed terms are often only offered so that your landlord can check if you are going to be a good tenant. Furthermore, if you have been happy and well cared for, legal requirements aside, courtesy still is useful. Remember, you may want to come back here for a reference, say for a future rental, or even for a mortgage application.

If you are terminating a tenancy, and you have almost no contact with your landlord or agent, it's always a good idea to register the letter. If there are any special terms or conditions in your lease, follow them. The leaving date you are giving is legally binding; you can't just change your mind if your new job falls through. If anything does happen within the formal notice period which makes you want to stay longer than your given leaving date, you need to contact the agency or landlord very quickly. If they have not already agreed a contract with someone else, they will probably be happy to work something out. Even if they have, and you have a track record of being a good tenant, the 'bird in the hand' theory will probably help you to persuade them. If they have found someone that they prefer however, perhaps even at a higher rent, you are unlikely to persuade them.

As soon as you give notice, you need to check your lease to find out what requirements have been put in for vacating the property, and there will be some. This is also an excellent time to remember that some landlords and agencies make significant profits from the cleaning and redecoration of properties when tenancies change hands. Some of the requirements that have been made may take a bit of time, but still need doing.

When you look at your lease, you are also likely to find in here a clause that allows, within reason, the landlord or agent to show prospective new tenants around the property during the notice period. Tenants who have got along well with their management may well be asked to 'tidy up a bit' when new tenants are viewing. OK, you're not obliged to do it, but if you've had a happy time, and you need a reference, it's not an unreasonable request.

If you are giving notice within the 'fixed term' its also very much in your interests to help your landlord find a new tenant as quickly as possible. Landlords are still obliged to 'take reasonable steps to find a suitable replacement' if this happens, and helping them out is a good idea. Some of the best services I know do genuinely try hard when tenants suddenly have to move out to try to reduce their tenant's potential losses, and as I have said before there are a large number of excellent landlords around.

Moving out

Before you leave, you must ensure that everything in the property is *exactly* as you found it. Here a well-organized inventory really comes into its own!

You need to clean thoroughly everywhere. It is no good taking a nice clean house or flat, and happily moving in for these reasons, and then leaving it in a less good condition. Take every room, clean every mark, wash every inch of floor (yes, even behind the loo). I know many landlords who always rent by preference to tenants who have been in the armed forces because they are marched into and out of all their service quarters under full inspection. Not all landlords want to make a few pounds washing up your mess. You need to defrost fridges, thoroughly clean cookers, and wash the *insides* of cupboards! Leave nothing to chance, or indeed charge. If it is a term of your lease and you signed it, you need to take drapes to the dry cleaners and provide a receipt. If linen has been provided, wash and iron it and leave it where you found it.

These are just the standard terms. Your own lease can have other requirements, and you need to observe them or you may be charged. Tenants in expensive units are advised to employ a professional cleaning service and save the receipt. And finally, replace anything you have broken or damaged to the same standard. You are actually required to leave the unit as you found it (genuine wear and tear excepted). Having cleaned thoroughly, replaced light-bulbs, etc., check around to make sure the furniture is in the same rooms as when you moved in. I know landlords who will shove an armchair back into the lounge, but agencies will call out the maintenance man. You have been warned.

If all this seems a little extreme, remember that the balance of responsibility is yours, not your landlord's or agent's. Whilst many are just delighted to get back a lovely clean property, and happy to return your deposit in exchange, sadly others are waiting for the tiniest detail for a deposit reduction. When you are satisfied, try and repeat the photo process in Chapter 4. This can seem like an awful trial I realize, but many of you will have lost money over this process in the past, and almost all of you will know someone else who has.

Final accounts

Don't forget to notify the gas and electricity companies of when you are leaving, and, as you move out, take a meter reading to check against your closing account. Tell the local authority, and the phone and water companies that you are leaving. So many tenants come badly unstuck with this process. Many really believe that if they don't admit to the authorities that they are living somewhere, they will get away without paying water rates, or community charges. In fact most reputable landlords and agents automatically provide the name and address of any new tenant to all the authorities, because unless the units are occupied, the *land-lord* is automatically billed. Provide everyone with a forwarding address for final accounts (these are an important part of the process for many deposit returns), and return the keys wherever requested.

Once you have left

Having left the property and given back the keys, you may find that some private landlords may inspect that day, and send your deposit to your provided forwarding address immediately. A few may even inspect just before you leave and pay you there and then, but this is rare.

Most agencies and private landlords, quite reasonably, not only check the building, but also ask for confirmation that you have settled all your final accounts before moving on. Given the number of tenants who try to leave behind a mountain of debts, this is a sensible precaution for managers to take. As well as the work involved, no new tenant wants to move into any property which has unpaid bills outstanding, or bad payment records. Each new tenant is entitled to a 'claim sheet'. Properties with records of County Court judgments recorded for debtors can be a nightmare to move in to, as no one will give the new tenants any credit either without immense amounts of work.

If you haven't paid your own bills, don't be surprised if your deposit is used to pay them.

The overwhelming majority of honest tenants who do pay their bills need to keep the paid counterfoils as proof, and to help speed up the return of the deposit. Some parties can be very slow in returning them. Don't forget your money is in accounts usually accruing interest which no one even asks for. Some people in the industry make margins at every opportunity!

Unfortunately, the length of time that (even within

reasonable practices) it takes to receive your original deposit back from one property, ready to use in order to make a move, can leave people trapped. If you are utterly dependent on the deposit held by one landlord to pay the deposit on the next, and you want to move from one to the other immediately (as most of us do), you can have real difficulty. The value of having a good relationship with your existing landlord is again obvious. However it's not always possible, and some landlords can be very oppressive about this. There are unfortunately no easy solutions to needing your deposit back from a bad landlord or agent, to enable you to move to something better. It really is a Catch 22 situation, which no amount of experience can really resolve, and one which bad practitioners can and regrettably do exploit, leaving tenants vulnerable and understandably frustrated.

There are two letters in Appendix 4 that you could find helpful if you are experiencing any difficulty in obtaining a deposit refund. The first is a polite letter to be copied out and posted together with the suggested proofs of payment fourteen days after you vacate, if you are still waiting. Enclose your proofs but keep photocopies. The second is a much stronger letter to be posted within fourteen days of the first, if you are still waiting. Once it ever becomes necessary to start writing for your deposit, you have reached the stage when you *must* register all letters so that you can prove that you have written.

Tenants who have returned the property they have been renting in good condition, and have proof that no outstanding bills remain unsettled, should have absolutely no hesitation in both threatening, and then taking action for its recovery in the Small Claims Court. These are inexpensive and effective. In most cases simply sounding well informed, and writing a letter that sounds competent, will be sufficient to concentrate the mind of whoever it is who is being slow. Your Citizens' Advice Bureau will write letters on your behalf, as will local law centres. If you have also made your own accurate provisions for proof (photos and witnesses), as suggested in Chapter 4, you will be even better protected.

9 When Your Landlord Tells You to Leave

The overwhelming majority of tenancies are terminated by tenants, giving written notice that they wish to leave the property. In a minority of cases, the landlord notifies the tenant that they require possession. Sometimes this is to reinforce the previous, perhaps verbal agreement they made with their tenant at the beginning of a 'fixed term', if they are not sure that the tenant is planning to leave. In a smaller number of cases it is simply because, for whatever reason, they want to have the property back.

These matters are quite complicated, and this section is intended for general information only about the broad framework of how things fit together. More detailed explanations are available in Chapter 15 'If Your Landlord Seeks Possession'. Two important things to remember are that no court will grant an order for possession to a landlord with a shorthold tenant until at least six months from the start of the original tenancy unless the tenant has breached a term of his tenancy, and provided the landlord has *grounds which can be proved*. No tenant is obliged to leave the property until the court grants a *possession order* which will state the date s/he must leave.

If your 'fixed term' is coming towards a close, so long as you are being given the statutory two months' written notification, you will not get a different decision from the court if you wish to pursue the matter, as the landlord is perfectly legally entitled to require possession and is exercising his automatic right. If you *had* a fixed term tenancy and this ended some time ago, the landlord can exercise this right at any time (again with two months' notice) into the statutory period. The six months protection you enjoyed started at the beginning of your original tenancy. He can also apply later than the 'fixed term' on a wider range of other grounds.

If you are still in your fixed term, the landlord can only apply to the court for a possession order on quite limited grounds. He cannot exercise his automatic right until the fixed term is expired (see Chapter 15). Any tenant in receipt of formal notice requiring possession is advised to seek further specialist advice from the CAB, or any of the previously suggested sources.

If you have a contractual periodic tenancy your landlord can apply to the court at any time from the start of the tenancy on a wide range of grounds. If he is exercising his automatic right however, he still cannot do so until six months have elapsed since the beginning of the tenancy. Again, you are entitled to two months' written notice for the automatic right. However with contractuals your landlord may be applying to the court on 'other grounds'.

Automatic rights of possession require at least two months' written notification. However, other applications for possession due to breaches of lease can be much shorter, from as little as two weeks. A full list together with the timescales involved is available in Chapter 15.

Some tenancies break down completely, and very acrimoniously. This is almost without exception because one party or another is behaving badly. It may be the last thing that someone wants to hear, but when things have reached this stage, it really often is the best thing to move on. Use the notice period to find somewhere else to live.

Sometimes, perfectly friendly tenancies are concluded because the 'fixed term' has expired, and the landlord wants to increase the rent. You may be unwilling or unable to now afford it, and the landlord will seek a new tenant.

What to do next

Don't assume however that because you have to leave that you need necessarily have further problems. Tenants who have been given notice can, if they have caused no damage, left no debts, and left the property in the same condition as they accepted it, fully expect, and are still legally entitled to, their deposit refund once all legitimate liabilities have been settled. Follow the advice in the previous chapter, and claim your refund.

This will obviously be more difficult if the landlord wants possession because you have damaged their property. Tenants who have lost their home because they have behaved badly should consider cutting their losses. Landlords with a possession order through the court, even if no further damage is done to their property, are able and often well advised to sue you in the county court. You could end up with the distinction of having lost your home, and your deposit, having to pay a fine and having a County Court judgement recorded against you. Hardly ideal, and rather difficult to find somewhere else to live, given the common use of tenant blacklists, and credit rating services.

On the other hand tenants told to leave without written notice, or worse ordered out should seek *immediate* advice from their local housing department, law centre or CAB. Your landlord simply cannot order you out, nor pack your things and move them out. All tenants, and a limited number of licensees even, still enjoy the legal right to stay in place until the *court* has granted a possession order. It remains the exclusive right of the court both to grant and enforce possession orders. At the bottom end of the market, some deeply disturbing things happen to tenants. These are covered in Chapter 14, 'Harassment and Illegal Eviction'.

10 Common Tenancy Types

For those of you wondering whether or not to bother reading this section, let me assure you that the following few pages of information are arguably the most important of the guide. If you haven't understood what you're being offered, or indeed have already signed, you have no hope at all of managing your tenancy!

Let us begin with a brief run through all the types of tenancies you might have heard of: assured tenancies; assured shorthold tenancies; regulated tenancies; part-protected tenancies; secure tenancies, etc. Now is the time to forget almost every type of tenancy you've ever heard of. You will not be offered most of them. Many, even if they still exist in law, would simply not be offered because they confer far too many rights on the tenant, given that there are alternatives that do not.

The best you are likely to be offered is an assured shorthold tenancy, and the worst will be a licence to occupy. Neither offer much real protection, but at least you have some limited security with an assured shorthold tenancy. With a licence you effectively have almost nothing. The only genuine remaining legal right a tenant enjoys is the right to not be evicted without a court order. As if that weren't little enough, if you occupy on a licence with a resident landlord often you don't even have that. Because of this, tenants need to be in a position to make informed choices before they embark on a let. With few meaningful rights, problem-solving during a let is hugely difficult.

What many people simply don't understand is that their rights (landlords and tenants alike) are determined not only by what is written on the paperwork both parties signed, but also by their relationship to one another. Tenants, imagining that they have a tenancy on a room, or house that they share with their landlord, may actually in fact only have a licence. This can be further complicated by the type of sharing of facilities which you have with your resident landlord. Similarly, landlords offering licences on rooms in properties which neither they nor other members of their family share with their tenants as their only or main residence will often find that, if challenged, courts will determine apparent licensees to be tenants.

Does it matter when I signed my licence/lease?

It can be crucial! Following the introduction of assured shorthold tenancies in 1988, many landlords and some agents did not comply with the strict requirement to serve the tenant with a Section 20 notice advising them that the tenancy was an assured shorthold. Despite everyone signing documents titled 'assured shorthold tenancies', unless the Section 20 was served before the tenancy agreement was signed, the tenancy created was in fact a straightforward assured tenancy, with extensive security of tenure inadvertently given to the tenants, often without either party realizing what they had accidentally created!

Recognizing the problem, revisions were put in place for *all tenancies starting on or after February 1997*, and now, unless otherwise quite specifically stated in writing, all tenancies are automatically assured shorthold tenancies.

What am I likely to be offered?

As stated before, you are almost invariably going to be offered either an assured shorthold tenancy, or a licence. We need to look at both in a little more detail. Any tenant who finds themselves confused in any way about the information in this section, or who finds that they are offered another, less common variant, must take some additional advice. Try your local Citizens' Advice Bureau, or a legal aid centre.

Many local authorities also have a dedicated private rented housing section, and many also have Tenancy Liaison Officers who specialize in giving advice to private tenants. The definitions given below are not intended to be comprehensive, but are a general guideline to the commonest forms that these tenancies can currently take.

Assured shorthold tenancies

Tenants do still enjoy some protection with this type of tenancy. The principal protection is that no tenant may be evicted without an order of the Court, and that landlords really do have to prove significant misbehaviour during the first six months of any assured shorthold tenancy, before a court will order a tenant to be evicted. Fuller details are available in Chapter 15.

You may be offered with what is known as a **'fixed term'** tenancy, the length of which is agreed between parties before signing. The advantage of a fixed term tenancy is that during that fixed term your landlord will only be able to seek possession through the courts on very limited grounds. Of course, if the tenant breaks any of the tenancy terms, the landlord can, and very often will, seek possession of their property on one of the grounds which are still available to him.

Even though the 1997 revisions in the law removed the previous requirement to offer a minimum fixed term tenancy of six months, thankfully it did not permit landlords to exercise their automatic right to possession in less than that time. You may find therefore that although you do not have a fixed term of six months, you still enjoy protection from possession for the first six months; naturally so long as you do not break any of the terms of your lease. In effect the change now means that, where it suits both parties to use an assured shorthold for, say, three months, it can be arranged, but landlords cannot abuse this.

You may be offered a **contractual periodic tenancy**, with no 'fixed term', where the tenancy runs from one rent period to another, say month to month or even week to week. These have the advantage of being very flexible for tenants because both parties can be equally restricted by fixed terms. If you have a fixed term of six months for example, and you want to move out in three, you can still be held responsible for the rent and other costs for the whole of the rest of that fixed term. However if your tenancy is a contractual periodic, and you need to move, this does not apply. However, during a contractual periodic tenancy, landlords can seek possession at any time and on a wider range of grounds than they could if you had a fixed term, where the grounds during that 'fix' are more restricted.

Your landlord still enjoys an automatic right of possession after six months with a contractual periodic tenancy, because it remains a basic principle of any assured *shorthold* tenancy that landlords may choose to terminate any time after the first six months, without a specific legal reason, provided that they have satisfied the legal requirements. This should not however concern responsible tenants, who still enjoy the benefits of the six-month rule.

Contractual periodics are relatively rare for reasons outlined below.

You may have a tenancy with an initial fixed term of say six months, and then both parties wish to continue the arrangement. In this case, one of two things may happen. Your landlord may offer you a brand new six month (or other) fixed term, which allows you both to 'renegotiate the terms of the tenancy' (which is usually double-talk for a rent increase). This does however give you a further whole six months' relative security.

Alternatively, your landlord may wish to continue the existing arrangement, and not want to renegotiate terms. This can be another very satisfactory arrangement. The existing tenancy will then automatically become a **statutory periodic tenancy**, which requires no further paperwork, and either party may now terminate the contract with proper notice, but neither party becomes tied to a further six months should their circumstances change.

Many sensible landlords use the initial fixed term to test the waters with new tenants. If they are happy with how things are progressing they are often very happy to allow statutory periodics to develop. They are however a little less likely to arise if your lease does not contain contingencies for, say, regular rent reviews, as the terms of the tenancy remain the original terms, and clearly long running statutory periods will require some agreement for future rent reviews. These are a little less likely through agencies, who often use the end of a fixed term to trigger a further lease extension fee.

Not surprisingly there are significant advantages, and significant disadvantages, with each of the options you are likely to encounter. Where contractual periodic tenancies offer flexibility if you are not happy, or want to leave for any other reason without being financially tied for a fixed period, they are often very difficult to negotiate. Few land-lords are really willing to offer the opportunity for you to walk away from a contract, leaving them with a potentially unlet unit and lost revenue for weeks, whilst you still, in effect (so long as you don't behave badly), enjoy relative security for the first six months.

From a landlord or agent's point of view, fixed terms make the tenant financially liable for the unit for at least the length of time that they are secure. The obvious disadvantage of a fixed term tenancy is exactly that which makes it so very attractive to their landlord! If you need to move on, even because the property proves most unsatisfactory, you can find yourself facing demands for rent on a unit you no longer live in.

Basically interpreted, a fixed term offers slightly more security to both landlord and tenant, and a contractual periodic offers slightly more flexibility. A statutory periodic arising after a fixed term has run for six months offers the same flexibility to both parties after the fixed term.

Despite assured and assured shorthold tenancies having quite clear terms and conditions for both landlords and tenants, you can occasionally find that your landlord has tried to vary the terms of the tenancy he is offering. For example, some landlords have tried to increase the length of written notice that a tenant is asked to provide when they want to leave the property, say once the fixed term has already expired. Landlords are not able to vary basic tenancy terms in this way simply by writing, 'Tenants are required to give two months' written notice of their intention to leave', where the legal requirement is in fact one month (or four weeks if the rent is paid weekly). Terms which landlords offer even in writing cannot 'conflict' with legislation, and indeed the legislation will automatically override what your landlord has unreasonably added. Tenants who find that they are being offered a standard pre-printed lease produced by a legal stationers, for example, or clearly drawn up by a solicitor, should find that the terms within it are in full compliance with the legislation. Do check carefully where your landlord has taken any lease and added a couple of obvious additions. If you're not sure about them, check with free sources of advice, like the CAB.

Oral agreements

Tenants and landlords may not even have a written agreement. The chances are that these tenancies (see 'Licences' section below also, if agreed since 28 February 1997, will now automatically be assured shorthold tenancies. It isn't what either you nor your landlord call your tenancy that is significant; its nature depends on the law of the land.

Some landlords prefer to not give anything in writing, often believing that they have more rights this way. This isn't the case for either party. It can be very hard for tenants to prove that they haven't agreed to a fixed term say of one year, which would allow their landlord or agency to pursue them for any rent or outgoings during this period unless they have something in writing. Both parties are much better protected with some written evidence of their contract.

Given tenants' vulnerability without written details of their oral tenancies, they are entitled in law to certain details in writing, if their tenancy began after 28 February 1997. Any tenant can make a written request to their landlord for the following details, and the landlord is obliged to provide within twenty-eight days a written confirmation of:

- The date the tenancy began.
- The amount of rent payable, and the dates on which it should be paid.

- Any rent review arrangements.
- The length of any 'fixed term' which has been agreed.

If your landlord refuses to provide this written statement or ignores your letter, you can get in touch with the local authority or the citizens' advice bureau, and they will help you. The landlord is actually liable to be fined if he won't provide you with this statement. For those of you who rent through agencies, and who have not been given the address of your landlord, write to the landlord via your agency. If the agent will not forward your written request for a statement, again contact one of the sources previously given, as you have a legal entitlement to be provided at least with the basic framework of your tenancy, and you are quite exposed without any written details.

Some tenants with oral tenancies which were agreed *before* February 1997, may in fact have the benefit of an assured tenancy, because, as was mentioned before, many landlords did not realize that by failing to serve a Section 20 notice on their prospective tenant before the tenancy began, they were automatically creating an assured tenant, with much more security. Again, what your landlord said can be much less significant than when they said it. If you think that this applies to you, make an appointment and take advice.

Licences

The single most important thing for inexperienced tenants to realize is quite how difficult it is for a landlord, who does not occupy the *same* property that you are offered a licence to live in, as his own or his family's main and only residence, to offer a licence at all! Far too often investors buy relatively large houses, and let to a variety of individuals on alleged licences. Anyone who has either a written or an oral agreement which has been called a licence would do very well to read the rest of this information and then seek advice again from any of the previous sources.

Quite often people find that they *in fact and in law* are tenants not licensees with far greater rights and securities than they had been led to believe. Again we are back to the fundamental point that the nature of your rights is not determined by anything other than the law of the land. Unfortunately licences are a great deal more difficult to define than tenancies, which is why you will need very specific advice on the very particular personal circumstances of your own licence to make sure it is genuine.

Landlords try to offer licences because the licensees have in effect almost no security. This obviously suits landlords very well, but is hardly ideal for tenants. Of course licences are a very reasonable proposition for landlords who themselves share either the whole, or just some parts of the same property and facilities with their licensees. It is a genuine safeguard for anyone to have control over the length of time someone shares one's own home. However, for a licence to be genuine at least some of the following criteria will need to apply to your circumstances.

- In the accommodation you agree to rent does your landlord live in the same building as his only, or main residence, or does another member of his family live there under these terms? If so you may have a valid licence.
- Do you occupy part of a converted house, e.g. a flat or bedsit, within a building where your landlord or another member of his family lives? This may be a licence.
- Do you have a fixed term you are obliged to stay? You may well have a tenancy.

- Do you share any facilities with your landlord, for example bathrooms, or kitchens? If so you may have a licence. If your sharing only applies to corridors or entrances, and you have exclusive use of some part of the building, you may have a tenancy.
- Are you provided with any services by your landlord? For example, are they or their staff able to enter your room on a very regular basis to clean? If so, you may have a licence. If, however, you basically look after yourself, and they empty the rubbish, or provide clean sheets each week, you may have a tenancy.
- Do you have exclusive use of any part of the building, into which no one else is allowed? You may have a tenancy. Even if your landlord lives downstairs this may offer you slightly more protection.

Perhaps it is easier to explain in the following way. If you live in a student hall of residence, with cleaning and catering, you usually have a licence. If you live in a hotel where staff clean and cater, you have a licence. Try to apply these criteria to your own circumstances. If they are a close match, and your landlord or a member of their family lives in the same building, you may very well have a genuine licence. This is however one of the most controversial areas of law and if you think that your circumstances don't seem to match these, talk to someone who can advise you.

You need specialist advice if you were offered a licence that you may by now be beginning to suspect may indeed be a tenancy, particularly if you have lived there since before 28 February 1997. Again the date is critical, because if you were offered a licence before that date, and you discover through advice that what you had indeed been granted was a tenancy, unless your 'landlord' served a Section 20 notice on you *before your tenancy began*, you may indeed not only have a genuine tenancy, that tenancy itself could be an assured tenancy in the same way as could have occurred in the preceding section over an acknowledged tenancy.

This is a very important distinction, as you would if this were the case now have the legal right to remain in your accommodation indefinitely, unless of course your landlord can prove in court that you have breached any of the grounds for possession outlined in Chapter 15. An assured tenancy is a valuable commodity, and you will find that you have access to advice through your local authority. If you don't find the advice clear, you can always try to obtain advice through a local solicitor. Many will offer half an hour's free advice through your local Citizens' Advice Bureau, and you may be entitled to some form of legal aid.

Perhaps in conclusion it might be added that whilst no one wants to advise people constantly to confront land-lords, to offer licences simply to deny people what are quite genuine rights is hardly a position anyone should want to encourage. Assured shorthold tenancies offer very consid-erable safeguards for landlords, which can sometimes be essential, but every form of earning one's income carries a small degree of risk and being a landlord is no exception. To offer licences as a mechanism for removing the very limited security which tenants now enjoy may seem to many people both inside and outside the industry to be a little excessive.

Who is responsible for repairs?

One of the most disputed areas between landlords/agents and tenants is that of who is responsible for what in terms of repairs.

In most cases, the following rules apply:

Landlord responsibilities

With an exception that is unlikely to affect any assured shorthold tenant or licencee (i.e. leases of longer than 7 yrs), all landlords have a statutory repairing obligation on them under the Landlord and Tenant Act 1985 for the following:

- The structure and exterior of the property, which usually includes drains, gutters and external pipes.
- Baths, basins, toilets, showers and other sanitary fittings.
- Heating, and hot water facilities.
- Gas and electrical services.

They are liable under different legislation for furniture safety, gas safety and for environmental health and fire safety requirements.

Before signing a lease, try to check that no unreasonable clauses about very expensive repairs and duties have been passed over to the tenant.

Tenant responsibilities

The tenant is under a legal obligation to behave in a tenant-like manner, and to conduct themselves in a way which will take care of the property.

- Turning off water or boilers, e.g. when going away in the winter if the heating is switched off.
- Mending fuses, replacing light bulbs, etc.
- Unblocking sinks, or other, which they have blocked with their own waste.

In addition tenants are responsible for not damaging the property, either deliberately or carelessly, and for ensuring that their guests don't either.

Remember, you cannot hold your landlord or agent responsible for the consequences of damage if you haven't notified them of a problem, and, especially if it is a serious problem, you would be well advised to do so in writing. Nor can you hold your manager responsible for damage to your own property if you have a problem which affects it, and you haven't bothered to let anyone know.

11   Understanding Your Lease

Often the leases that assured shorthold tenants are offered come from a standard legal stationers. These are usually obvious, with the name of the legal stationers clearly stated (generally on the back page). Alternatively, you could be presented with a standard lease, prepared by your agent's lawyers – these too will usually be titled. The third alternative is a specific lease on several typed pages, drawn up by a solicitor engaged by the landlord. Often too these will have the name of the firm somewhere obvious at the beginning or the end.

If your lease is one of these, a degree of confidence can be felt. If there is no sign on the lease that it has been drawn up by a qualified professional, try to stall and ask for time to read the lease. You still have the option of showing it to someone at the CAB, to check nothing either unusual or too onerous has been popped in.

Standard terms

Here is a short breakdown, and a little exploration of some (but not by any means all) of the clauses you may find. It is however only designed to give a general, rather than a legal, interpretation of what they may mean.

'A term certain of . . .' is normally found on a fixed term

tenancy. The landlord or agent will fill in here six months, or nine months, etc. This then is usually the length of your 'fixed term', where you enjoy the greatest security. Unless you find something specific on your lease, the rent will then usually be for the duration of the 'fixed term'. Break clauses, giving either party a right to terminate before the 'fixed term' end, are normally written into leases. Rent reviews at (say) six-monthly or yearly intervals are normally included in the lease. If they have not been written into the lease, no specific provision has been made for them. Wording might therefore be 'the landlord lets, and the tenant takes the property for the term, at the rent . . .'.

References to the property include reference to any 'part or parts of' the property, and the 'furniture, fixtures' etc., usually incorporates tenant liability for everything that comes with the property, and that is incorporated on the inventory, as well as the actual structure.

Some terms are obvious, they cover rent payments, accepting responsibility for gas, electricity, water and sewerage charges, and usually commit you to liability for local authority taxes.

Tenants will often see terms like, 'yield up the property at the end of the tenancy', which means, in simple terms, return to the landlord or agent.

Some leases have a clause which insists that tenants do nothing which 'vitiates' insurance. This means to make invalid, or ineffectual, a landlord's insurance. This might mean bringing in paraffin or other portable heaters which are prohibited by your landlord's insurers, or messing about with the electrics and causing fires. It could also mean ensuring that the building is kept secure (i.e. locked). These clauses are often not entirely specific, they are meant to be quite wide to offer some security for the landlord's considerable investment.

'Make good pay for or repair or replace' places a responsibility upon tenants to return the property and contents in the same operational or decorative condition that they were in when you moved in. Usually a statement that reasonable wear and damage by fire are excepted is also included.

Some leases specifically instruct tenants to return all furniture to the positions there were in on acceptance of the property. There is also a very common lease requirement to wash all linens 'soiled during the tenancy'. Where tenants see this they should apply common sense. If you feel it necessary to clean the curtains don't put your landlord's expensive drapes through the launderette! Check what is being required with the management, and then comply with it.

'No pets' is very typical, and this does include hampsters as well as St Bernards.

Commonly here there will be specific lease obligations, for example: 'not sublet', which means don't move someone else in to help pay part of the rent; 'assign', which means not to move elsewhere, and give the property to anyone else; 'receive paying guests', without the landlord's specific written *prior* consent (which means *before* you do it, not afterwards when the landlord or agent finds out). Your use of any rented housing is usually confined specifically to normal residential use. You cannot then carry out any business without prior written consent.

'Permit the landlord or the landlord's agents' (which can mean the lettings agent, or the landlord's employees for example) 'to enter the property to view the condition', is usually accompanied by the condition of 'at reasonable hours'. The landlord would usually be expected to give twenty-four hours' notice of this. 'To enter in case of emergency', or 'reserves right of entry for emergencies', would reasonably allow a landlord to enter without necessarily being obliged to give notice, if for example there was a serious problem which couldn't wait twenty-four hours, like a burst pipe. This does not of course cover straightening the curtains, as mentioned before.

Very commonly the lease will contain a clause which 'permits the landlord or their agents to enter and view the property with prospective tenants'. This is usually restricted to 'at reasonable hours, within the last twenty-eight days of the tenancy. By observing all the lease requirements, and paying their rent as agreed, the tenant buys a right to 'quiet enjoyment'. This should be free of all unreasonable interference and interruption from the landlord, or by anyone claiming to represent or indeed actually representing them.

12 How Your Landlord's Mortgage Can Affect You

During the eighties, some press coverage about this issue started to filter out. The lettings business was booming because no one could sell their house, and negative equity (where your house is worth less than you paid for it), hit hundreds of thousands of homeowners. Although the issue has gone off the media boil now, the fact that your landlord might have borrowed money to buy the house you're living in can have some interesting effects on you.

Most rented property is bought with borrowed money. Special deals for investment in rented property have suddenly emerged, and newspapers are filled with articles encouraging new landlords into the field. This is absolutely great, and is where most new rentals have come from. However, even if you dutifully pay your rent, some landlords don't dutifully pay their mortgages. A debt can still be building up against the property, with legal consequences which can literally mean you losing your home, despite it not being your fault in any way. Of course, this doesn't happen too often, but if it affects you, the fact that you are in a minority doesn't make you feel any better. To a certain extent this is a risk you take, however being completely unaware that it exists doesn't seem completely sensible.

Actually almost all normal mortgages have a clause in

them which prohibits the borrower subletting without authority from the lender (bank, building society). Many landlords completely ignore this, and rent away. For the majority this causes absolutely no problem, as the owner uses the rent to pay the mortgage and no one is any the wiser. It is a little different when the landlord is in financial difficulty and doesn't keep paying their mortgage. As the number of repossessions (where the lender goes to court for a possession order) is again slowly creeping back up, tenants can sometimes have real problems. In theory, anyone who has borrowings against a property they are letting out should serve a special notice, called 'Prior Notice', on their tenants advising them that the lender may want to sell it (see Chapter 15), but in practice many don't bother. Sometimes landlords are not being deliberately misleading. You actually have to know quite a bit about the lettings industry even to be aware of this rule. Like all lettings rules, it gets broken mainly because it's difficult to enforce.

Any tenant can find out if their landlord has a mortgage. If you want to find out, you can fill out a special form from the HM Land Registry nearest to the property (form 109). Currently the charge is only four pounds and the Land Registry are helpfully turning these around in about forty-eight hours. Whilst it won't tell you if your landlord is in financial difficulty, the name of the lender will be on this document. At least with the name of the lender in your file, you have a chance of trying to sort this out if you become aware of problems.

Unfortunately, often the first thing a tenant knows is that a possession order has been issued through the courts from the lender. Most tenants do find out at least at this stage, because there is often an agreement that the possession order be addressed to the landlord and all occupants, which does mean you are able to open it, even if you don't like what you read. Where this doesn't happen, the court will usually try to make sure something similar does, as they are aware that tenants do sometimes live in properties which are subject to possession orders. The alternative would be that the court process would be completed and the bailiffs possibly arrive before an unsuspecting tenant even realized what was happening.

If you do ever find yourself in these circumstances you must act very quickly. If a possession order does come through your door it will have the date that the possession becomes effective already on it. If you have been aware for some time that financial difficulties surround your land-lord, you may already have applied through the county court on a form N224 to be 'joined to the proceedings'. This means that although you still won't be able to stop the possession, you may be given a little extra time in which to find somewhere else to live before the locks are changed.

In any of these circumstances don't just sit around worrying, or hoping the situation will somehow disappear. It is already deeply serious once lenders begin taking action. Make an immediate appointment with your local Citizens' Advice Bureau, legal aid centre, or local council. Here staff have experience which you need to help you retrieve the best from what are truly awful circumstances. They may help you with legal paperwork, or even ask the landlord's lender at least to give you time to find new accommodation.

Tenants in this position lose out in every aspect. Deposits have been paid, and rent duly delivered, and in truth may be lost. Theoretically you can take legal action against your landlord, because he owes you money, and you may even be entitled to compensation. However it can be very diffi-cult indeed, especially if you don't have your landlord's current address. Discuss all these matters with whomever you have approached for guidance.

13   Can My Rent Be Raised?

Ideally, these issues should have been thrashed out before you signed your contract. However it is really quite rare that tenants ask what rent increases are likely to apply in the future. Perhaps they imagine that if they ask, it will encourage the landlord to start thinking about it too! Although landlords are not supposed to increase your rent more than about once a year, if they do, and the first six months of your tenancy have elapsed, in reality you have the same recurring problem that applies to all the terms of these tenancies. If you challenge it, your landlord still enjoys his automatic right of possession with two months' notice. For many tenants this is therefore theoretical, rather than practical information, providing an overview of a few common scenarios.

Fixed term tenancy

Usually the agreement will state that the rent will be fixed for the length of 'the fix' i.e. six, nine or twelve months. It may however 'fix' the rent for six months and then say it will be reviewed at certain intervals. If it does say this, then the rent can go up. If you don't want to agree to pay higher rent in the future, don't sign a lease that commits you to it in advance.

If the landlord or agent wants to increase it by more than it states in the lease, you must agree either to pay it, or not.

Do remember, if you decline, you are unlikely to have your lease extended.

If you have a fixed term and a lease which does not mention rent increases, your rent can only be raised during the fixed term if you agree. If you disagree the landlord has to wait until the end of whatever length 'fix' was signed.

Your landlord may not propose this method of increase however. Some landlords and agents offer a new fixed term, and a new rent level, every six months. These you must either accept, or decide to move, because they are effectively whole new tenancies every time, and the landlord can ask for whatever rent they please, Rent Assessment Committee permitting.

Contractual periodic tenancy

Your landlord should give you at least a month's notice in writing of any proposed increases in rent, usually using a special form called 'Landlord's Notice Proposing a New Rent under an Assured Periodic Tenancy or Agricultural Tenancy'. If you receive one of these you have two choices. Either pay the increase, or refer the new proposed rent to the Rent Assessment Committee, but do remember the warning given earlier, and do some checking up before you make an application to an R.A.C. If you decide to do this, you need to apply before the date the increased rent is due. Further increases can come each year.

Statutory periodic tenancy

If your fixed term has expired and you and your landlord want to consider continuing the tenancy, the landlord may want to increase your rent. This can be done in writing, or by using the form mentioned above, under contractual periodic tenancies. Again you have the same choices as previously, and further increases can arise each year the tenancy continues.

Licences

Genuine licences are in reality much more flexible arrangements between parties than tenancies. If you have a licence, all the terms need to be arranged between yourself and your landlord. Given their almost complete lack of security, landlords are able to ask for rent increases in whatever way is worked out between the parties. Licensees have no formal mechanism for redress. Simply, if the rent reaches a level which you feel is too high, your only genuine strategy is to look for a more reasonably priced unit.

N.B. Tenancies beginning after February 1997 have some restrictions on the number and timing of applications from tenants to the R.A.C. If your tenancy has been granted since this date, before you even consider making an application, telephone the R.A.C. and ask for advice.

14   Harassment and Illegal Eviction

Harassment

Whilst it seems extraordinary to most of us (even those who don't exactly like our landlords and agents much), there is still a considerable distinction between practitioners who aren't very reasonable, and the landlords whose conduct will be considered here. For some tenants it can be such a huge problem that the guide would not be complete without its inclusion. Whilst it may not affect a very high proportion of tenants, its effects can be utterly devastating, and some of the tenants affected have the types of tenancies which this guide has been designed to examine.

There is legislation in place: the Protection From Eviction Act, 1977. Further protection also exists for tenants under the 1988 Housing Acts. Although the offences are criminal, it isn't the police usually, but the local authority who will prosecute these crimes. If a landlord is found guilty he can receive a heavy fine, and/or a prison sentence.

Harassment can take many forms. Although it can be because your landlord has a dispute with you, or is racist, or doesn't like your private life, the main cause of harassment is of course money. It most often seems to happen to people who get behind with their rent, or if the landlord could make more money from the building if the tenant left.

Whatever the motivation, its effects are often appalling. Here are a few to consider:

- Landlord's workmen doing work to the property over a very long time and in a way to maximize inconvenience.
- Landlords or their staff barging in and out of the property uninvited and very often.
- Having the landlord's friend or relative move into the next flat and play loud music constantly.
- Shouting and swearing abuse at tenants.
- Changing the locks so tenants can't get into their home.
- Turning off the water, gas or electricity.
- Stealing your mail.
- Taking your possessions from your home.
- Sexual or racial abuse.

Whilst working in a South London centre for the elderly, I was called out to an emergency. A lady in her late seventies lived in the top flat of a run down 4-storey house. I had a key, and went straight up. Her flat was devastated. Large slabs of heavy old lath-and-plaster ceiling were everywhere, some almost a metre across. The landlord had taken off the roof slates several months ago to encourage her to move. If she hadn't actually been in the loo at the time the ceiling finally collapsed, she would have been dreadfully hurt. This woman had never owed a penny to anyone in her life, she was just trying to live in the home she had had since the war. The landlord had bought an investment property in an area of rapid gentrification. She was just in the wrong place at the wrong time.

Of course, as the number of secure tenancies has declined, some of these stories have reduced, but some tenants still have despotic landlords. Even with automatic rights of possession, some landlords can behave appallingly if, say, tenants fall behind with their rent. If your landlord is behaving in any way that makes you uncomfortable (as opposed to irritated), get in touch with the tenancy relations officer at your local council. They will help, and there are laws to protect you.

Illegal eviction

This is usually easier for a tenant to substantiate because it is clearer in many ways. It is an eviction which is not lawful, and for most tenants that means eviction by the landlord or his employees without a court order. This is the 'suitcases in the garden' syndrome I referred to in the introduction.

You can actually be evicted illegally from just a part of your accommodation. For example if the landlord locks off rooms in a house you are renting to deprive you of their use, a not-uncommon trick I'm afraid: 'You owe me some rent, I'm taking some space back till you've paid up.'

Even if the landlord has an absolute possession order (see 'Grounds for Possession'), he cannot simply walk in and turf you out. If he has an order, and you haven't moved out by the date on the order, the landlord cannot personally evict tenants. He must seek a warrant for eviction from the court, who will send bailiffs to evict.

In this depressing section there is one more thing I need to mention, although I hope it affects none of my readers. Although the action for both the above is taken by the local authority, if your landlord, or anyone working for them ever threatens violence, or is violent, you must contact the police, not the local authority. Sometimes they can be a little reluctant to get involved, but if you do feel under any sort of physical threat, only the police may act.

15 If Your Landlord Seeks Possession

Whilst this is a complex area, the following information is provided to enable you to have at least a little understanding of this process. Any tenant who finds themselves in this situation *must* take immediate specialist advice on their own particular circumstances, and should not rely on the information here which is for guidance only.

'Grounds' are in essence legal reasons. A list of all the grounds which apply to these tenancy types, together with the periods of written notice you are entitled to, follow. However, in all cases, whatever the grounds for possession, and however long or short the notice period must be, the landlord is always obliged to give the tenant a form of written notice. No tenant can find that they have lost their home without any prior knowledge.

As stated before, once six months, or the fixed term has elapsed, any landlord with an assured shorthold tenant may apply for possession of their property. If this is the only reason for their application, they are obliged to give the tenant two months' written notice of their intention to apply to the court.

For those tenants with a 'fixed term' that has still not expired, your landlord can only apply to the court for possession on grounds 2, 8, 10, 15 and 17, and only if the tenancy agreement made provision for it.

For tenants with contractual periodic tenancies with no fixed term, your landlord may apply for possession at any time during that tenancy on any of the grounds available to him/her. If your landlord serves notice in these circumstances, the landlord needs to make the last day of the tenancy, the last day of a tenancy period, i.e. the day before your next rent would be due.

There are two basic types of possession order: **absolute possession order**, where the court orders possession on one of the mandatory grounds, and **suspended possession orders**, where a discretionary ground has been used, and the court may decide to allow the tenant to stay on, so long as they meet the conditions set down by the court. If these conditions are breached, clearly your landlord can go back to court.

Accelerated possession procedures can be used by landlords to speed up the legal process, but only if the tenant has a written tenancy agreement (including statutory periodics), and your landlord has given you the appropriate written notice. These accelerated possession orders may be applied for if your landlord is trying to gain possession on Grounds 1, 3, 4 or 5. There are special rules that apply, and tenants in receipt of these should *seek legal advice.*

Grounds for possession

A 'ground' is a legal reason. A mandatory ground is one where the court must grant a possession order to the landlord. A discretionary ground is one where the court *may* grant a possession order to the landlord.

Some of these grounds require prior notice to have been served on the tenant before the tenancy was agreed, in order to forewarn tenants that the landlord might apply to the court.

Mandatory grounds

Ground 1
That the landlord gave the tenant written notice at the start of the tenancy that they used to live in the property as their only, or main home. (Or, in certain circumstances, that they or their wife require it to live in as their main home).

Ground 2
That the landlord has served a prior notice on the tenant at the beginning of the tenancy stating that they used to live in the property as their only or main home, and the property was subject to a mortgage granted before the tenancy started and that the lender wants to sell it, usually to pay off mortgage arrears.

Ground 3
That the tenancy is for a fixed term not exceeding eight months, and at sometime during the twelve months before the tenancy started, the property was let or licensed for a holiday.

Ground 4
A notice was served on the tenant at the start of the tenancy, and the tenancy is a fixed term tenancy not exceeding twelve months, that at some time during the twelve months before the tenancy began the property was let by a specified educational establishment to students.

Ground 5
A notice was served on the tenant at the beginning of the

tenancy stating that the property is held for use by a minister of religion, and is now required for that purpose.

Ground 6
The landlord intends to demolish or redevelop the property and cannot do so with the tenant living there. (This ground cannot be used where the landlord can do the work around the tenant without them having to move, nor can it be used where the landlord or someone before them bought the property with an existing tenant, usually a sitting tenant. The tenant's removal expenses have to be met.

Ground 7
The former tenant who must have had either a contractual or statutory periodic, has died in the previous twelve months, and no one living at the property has a right to succeed to the tenancy.

Ground 8
The tenant owes at least two months' rent, or eight weeks if the rent is weekly based, at the time the landlord served notice, and this amount is still outstanding at the date of the court hearing.

Discretionary grounds

Ground 9
Suitable alternative accommodation is available for the tenant or will be from the date the order takes effect (the Housing Act 1988 defines suitable alternative accommodation). The tenant's removal costs will be met.

Ground 10
The tenant was behind with the rent, both when notice of

seeking possession was served, and when court proceedings began.

Ground 11
Although the tenant was not behind with his rent when the landlord started possession proceedings, they have been persistently late with their rent.

Ground 12
The tenant has broken one or more of the terms of their tenancy agreements, except the obligation to pay rent.

Ground 13
The condition of the property has become worse because of the behaviour of the tenant, their sub-tenant, or any other person living there.

Ground 14
The tenant, or someone living with the tenant, or visiting the tenant, has caused, or is likely to cause, a nuisance or annoyance to other persons living in, or visiting the locality; or that any of them have been convicted of using the property or allowing it to be used for immoral, or illegal purposes, or have committed an arrestable offence in or in the locality of the property.

Ground 15
The condition of the furniture has become worse, because it has been ill-treated by the tenant, their sub-tenant, or someone else living in the property.

Ground 16
The tenancy was granted because the tenant was employed by the landlord, or a former landlord, and the tenant is no

longer employed by the landlord.

Ground 17
The landlord was persuaded to grant the tenancy on the basis of a false statement made knowingly or recklessly by the tenant or any person acting at the tenant's instigation.

Where any of these grounds are applied to you seek immediate legal advice on receipt.

Notice periods for each ground

For grounds: 3, 4, 8, 10, 11, 12, 13, 15 and 17, at least two weeks' notice is required.
For grounds: 1, 2, 5, 6, 7, 9 and 16, at least two months' notice is required.

Ground 14 has been strengthened by the 28 February 1997 revisions. Landlords may start proceedings as soon as they have served notice. All notices should state the grounds that the landlord is intending to base his application upon. There is no specific 'ground' for automatic possession rights of landlords.

16 Houses in Multiple Occupation

Until quite recently, despite always being quite controversial, a number of assumptions had been made about houses which were being let to several individuals. Houses in multiple occupation are defined under the 1985 Act: 'a "house in multiple occupation" means a house which is occupied by persons who do not form a single household'. This definition is what is currently under challenge.

Previously, local environmental health departments were able to serve notices for what they considered reasonable safety standards on a number of properties up and down the country, where they believed that the individuals (even where they had all signed one lease on occasions), in fact did not make up one household and standards were deficient.

Recently however, in a famous legal judgement, the Court of Appeal made a judgment at variance with what had previously been understood by many councils. In this landmark judgement, it was ruled that a relatively small number of students involved with this notice, did not enjoy this protection, because, in this case, the landlord proved that they could be defined as one household.

This judgement has caused considerable problems for councils up and down the country. Students in particular are often housed in some of the cheapest and often the worst accommodation in university towns. In addition, their desire to rent in groups for economy makes them vulnerable to living in what are technically overcrowded conditions.

Shared houses

Where most local authorities only served notices in circumstances where they were genuinely concerned (i.e. if the tenants weren't perhaps a natural friendship group who would look out for one another) it was still widely believed, until the Sheffield case, that they enjoyed protection. Since this case, councils up and down the country 'may be wary of attempting to use their powers in shared student houses' because 'the position of houses shared by groups of students is often uncertain' (the Department of the Environment, Transport and the Regions, October 1998).

This is a truly worrying situation, especially since students are without question, in the main, very inexperienced tenants, and pretty impoverished. That of all groups they should find themselves so apparently exposed is most unsatisfactory. In addition to this, given how the news of legal precedents spreads quickly, many landlords are challenging many other notices served on them, in an attempt to stretch the boundaries of the law. This, unless action is taken, will result in a completely unsatisfactory situation in every respect.

The government is currently working to consult on a possible national licensing scheme to cover many of the properties which are shared or multi-occupied. However, until then, the practice of putting any group of sharers under one lease, in the hope of avoiding any legitimate safety regulations, is spreading fast. At the time of writing therefore the situation for students in particular, and sharers in general, is pretty bleak.

Houses let in rooms or converted houses

There is a difference between say a three-bedroomed semi being let to students, friends, or colleagues, and a larger house which is let off in separate parts to people who don't know each other. If therefore you rent a room or a bedsit, you may be slightly safer, although undoubtedly the Sheffield case will also be used here to try again to stretch the law further. This type of accommodation can vary from the truly excellent, with every safety facility which could sensibly be required, to the rat runs which we all have heard about. Basically, tenants should try themselves to make some attempt to establish if their accommodation is safe. Safety is even more important here, where individuals come and go independently. Who is going to know for example if you are in or out in the event of a fire? Furthermore, where individuals do let parts of a property, the individual rooms are often locked, making escape even more hazardous.

Registration schemes

The government has recently introduced the option for local councils to introduce compulsory registration schemes for these types of properties (or those that it knows about or which have been declared).

If you want this type of accommodation, your local council have lists of safe properties in their areas. Other local councils have gone even further, and have also introduced (sometimes in conjunction with student accommodation services) an accreditation system, where landlords offering facilities beyond the legal minimum can be found. Don't rent this type of property without at least checking what is available that is safe in your own town. This registration seems to be the forerunner to a compulsory, and much needed, national licensing scheme for landlords.

For those of you who now live, or are considering living in shared or multi-occupied buildings, here is a list of what a registration scheme is likely to insist upon. It isn't exhaustive, some councils' requirements differ, but it is a guide.

Management requirements

A duty to keep the building in reasonable order, maintaining fire precautions and fire escapes, and hall lighting, and a notice of who the manager is and where they can be contacted. In addition they are usually required to maintain water, drainage, rubbish clearance, etc.

Gas and electricity

The management will be required to satisfy the local council that gas and electrical supplies are safe, and regularly checked.

Fire safety

Depending on the circumstances (especially the number of floors), a fire alarm may be required, heat detectors and sometimes emergency lighting for means of escape are required. Fire doors on escape routes are required. Buildings which have more than five storeys often need a second means of escape, perhaps a second emergency stair facility. Fire spread between floors is often sought. Fire extinguishers and fire blankets are usually required.

Amenities

Usually not less than one bath/shower per five occupants, and this to be no more than one floor away from each let unit. Reasonable hot/cold water supplies to above, plus ventilation, and adequate lighting. They should also be easy to keep clean. Not less than one toilet per five occupants, and again not more than one floor distant from you. Hand basins in or near toilets. Kitchens with adequate hot/cold water. Work surfaces, a fridge and reasonable cooking facilities. One kitchen between either three or five occupants, depending on the size of the accommodation. A minimum number of power points.

Reading this list, you may be as concerned as many connected to the industry that there is even minority dispute that these basic facilities and safety requirements should be provided for tenants, but there is. If your building has these basic requirements, it is probably much safer than the huge number which do not. You as a tenant ought to familiarize yourself with them, and try to find a property with one of the many responsible landlords who have already paid for their installation. I can assure you, responsible landlords are every bit as cross that having invested thousands of pounds to ensure their own tenants' safety, a minority of their colleagues seem to find them such an outrageous imposition. Interestingly, the rent levels charged do not seem to vary very much either; it seems that tenants don't really vote with their feet as often as they might.

Appendix 1
Checklist of Dos and Don'ts

Do

- Check carefully where you want to live, and for how long, before you sign leases.
- Do all your sums carefully, and be sure you can afford the total cost before you sign leases.
- Check at least basic safety in your own accommodation.
- Remember, you take the property 'as seen', don't ask for a string of improvements unless they are safety related.
- Make sure you have the money available for the deposit, and advance rent and all other advance charges before you agree to take a property.
- Register for council tax, water, electricity, gas, etc. Check meters when you move in and out and keep records.
- Get an exemption certificate from your college if you are a student exempt from council tax. Don't just not pay it, you'll end up with a summons that way.
- Check that your own possessions are insured, your landlord's policy probably won't cover them.
- Report anything that breaks down immediately, and in writing if necessary.
- Be reliable with your rent, and keep a record of all payments.
- Replace anything you have damaged or broken.

- Look after your landlord's property, remember you are only renting its use.
- Make sure your guests behave.

Don't

- Hand over any money unless you're certain you want this particular property.
- View properties alone unless absolutely unavoidable.
- Authorize builders, plumbers, etc., to carry out work to the property without written consent, your landlord will probably refuse to reimburse you.
- Do any damage, and try to pretend you're not liable.
- Imagine no one will know you live there, and hope you won't have to pay your way. Most landlords and agents notify every service provider anyway.
- Give keys of copies of keys to anyone else.
- Invite your boy/girlfriend to live with you without your landlord's consent. The property was only let to the signatories of the lease, and you cannot freely invite others. Joint leases made between four tenants cannot be extended to more than four without consent.
- Change the people living on joint tenancies without notifying the management. You may end up with no lease at all.

Appendix 2
Useful Tips

Having read this guide, it must now be obvious that every part of the letting process is interdependent on the other. Choosing the right property, and trying to find, and knowing what to look for in a good landlord are perhaps the most important of the choices you are trying to make. Many of the problems of poor conditions, unsafe properties, or unfair deposit retentions have the same core of agents and landlords in common. You might find the following suggestions useful.

- Read up on the information about registered landlords in Chapter 17, especially if you are looking to rent at the lower end of the price range, or if there is a group of you.
- Student accommodation services will provide lists of accommodation for sharers, but not all universities insist their landlords have the same standards required by your local council.
- Ask outgoing tenants what the landlord is like before you move in. Pop back in the evening when the landlord or agent isn't around, the answer could be very interesting, and it is usually well worth the trouble.
- If your friends or acquaintances like their landlord or their agent, take the phone number. Many of the best

have discreet waiting lists or choose tenants by recom-
mendation, for obvious reasons. Some of the best never
have to advertise at all.

- If you're looking to rent a room in a house, consider
  choosing one where the owner actually lives. Your legal
  rights may be limited, but the building is more likely to
  be safe. Many of the worst fire traps have absent landlords who live in a nice safe place up the road!
- If problems with the conduct of your landlord or
  tenant do arise after you have moved in, *take advice*.
  Don't just struggle on hoping things will get better,
  they may get worse. Find out where you stand, even
  six months can be a very long time with problematic
  management.

Unfit property

If you are living now, or have recently been living in, any
property which you would like to report to the authorities,
but dare not whilst you live there, here is some advice.
Once you have left, but *only when you have received your
deposit return*, write a letter detailing your concerns, and
post it (even anonymously) to the environmental health
department of your local council, who will, with a written
complaint, usually inspect promptly.

If every tenant living in unsafe or unfit accommodation
reported it, even after they had left, the number of these
units would go down very rapidly. Remember, *you* may
have found something better, but someone else has just
moved in!

Many times these type of properties are *wholly unknown
to the authorities*. How can they know if tenants don't tell
them? Landlords aren't going to. Some landlords can keep

a remarkably low profile if declaring their business will cost them money!

Appendix 3
Basic Safety

Here is a list of basic safety tips and hints which you might consider before you make your choices on where to live.

- Make sure that the upholstered furniture has a British Standard label.
- Never take a rented property which doesn't have gas safety certificates for the appliances. Also check out these warning signs: old style gas water-heaters in the bathroom or kitchen; a smell of fumes from any gas appliance; soot or staining on the gas fire or a boiler.
- Never try to save money by blocking ventilation grilles, they have often been installed to supply your gas appliance with sufficient air for safety.
- Don't take property where portable gas or paraffin heaters are provided, especially as your only source of heating.
- Look for smoke alarms, fire extinguishers and fire blankets.
- In large buildings look for fire alarms, fire doors, etc.
- Look for old electrical services and appliances. Do the lights flicker? Are there old style sockets? Do the heaters or kettles have old cables, or bare bits of wire?

There is now considerable publicity about gas safety certificates, and gas safety generally. What is often far less well publicized is that you can be equally poisoned by carbon monoxide from coal and smokeless fuel, even wood. So, a solid fuel boiler that isn't required to have a special certificate can still be a problem. It's also a great deal more difficult to see signs of dangerous sooting on a fire, because you expect it to a greater extent!

If you are concerned, here are a few symptoms of carbon monoxide poisoning which could alert you to a problem: tiredness, drowsiness, headaches, dizziness and nausea.

If you are concerned, you must report to your landlord or agent that day. Do not use any appliance you are worried about until it has been checked. You can buy small domestic testers to use at home if you are in any way concerned.

Appendix 4
Deposit Return Letters

One of the single largest areas of dispute between landlords and tenants is that of deposit returns. This can be difficult for well-meaning tenants, who do everything that they imagine is required, and still don't receive a deposit return after vacating the property.

Two letters are provided in this appendix to help tenants in this situation. The first letter is a polite request for a refund, showing what to mention, and that the tenant should ask for the interest on their deposit to which they are entitled. The second is a more formal demand for a refund, to be used by tenants who are, as is all too common, being ignored.

Follow the instructions and fill in the blanks. If you are entitled to a refund, knowing what to say, when, and to whom, is very useful. Whilst a landlord with good cause will happily go to court over the issue, less scrupulous landlords often perceive your deposit as additional income, and are reluctant to return it. Well-informed tenants are less likely to fall victim to this quite unacceptable practice.

First deposit return letter

Tenant's name
Tenant's address

Name of landlord or agent
Address of landlord or agent

Date

Dear (fill in)

re: (fill in the full address of the property you have vacated)

I was a tenant in the above property from (insert date) to (insert date). You held during my tenancy a deposit against damage amounting to (insert amount held as deposit).

I vacated the property as agreed, and returned the property in the condition required. I enclose (list here any receipts you have in connection with your final cleaning, if any).

I enclose for your attention my paid final receipts covering gas, electricity, telephone, water rates and council tax (add any other accounts for which you accepted responsibility).

I should be grateful if you could arrange for my deposit, together with the interest now due on the monies held by yourself for the period of my tenancy to be posted to me at my new address above, at your earliest convenience.

Yours sincerely

(Your signature)

(Your name)

Send to landlord or agent *recorded delivery* fourteen days after vacation, and don't forget to enclose the receipts referred to in the letter.

Second deposit return letter

Tenant's name
Tenant's address

Name of landlord or agent
Address of landlord or agent

Date

Dear (fill in)

re: (fill in the address of the property you have vacated)

I refer to my letter of the (fill in date of first letter), to which I have received no reply despite recording its delivery.

You have by now been provided with all the necessary documentation to enable you to release my deposit, but have failed thus far to do so. The sum currently outstanding is (fill in amount of deposit), plus the accrued interest to the date of this letter.

I must now formally advise you that, both on moving into the property, and on vacation of the same I took the precaution of (here outline in detail the precautions you took to safeguard your deposit, either the witnesses you had, or your recorded envelope of unopened proof – see Chapter 5 for ideas).

Unless therefore you have evidence to the contrary, I should be most obliged if you could now repay my deposit, in full and without further delay. Please send me receipts for any deductions you have made, plus a full written statement of the reasons for any such deductions.

Unless I am in receipt of all outstanding monies within seven days from the date of this letter I reserve the right, without further notice, to initiate a summons for their recovery through the small claims court.

Yours sincerely

(Your signature)

(Your name)

Post to landlord or agent *recorded delivery* within fourteen days of the first letter.

Appendix 5
Helpline Services

Many tenants will feel that, even with this guide, there are occasions when they would like to discuss a particular matter that has arisen during their tenancy. Indeed, advice before you make a decision on something you are not sure about can be invaluable.

Whilst the suggested sources of information in this book, such as the CAB, local authorities, etc., are excellent, sometimes, due to heavy workloads, the practical advice you need may take a little time to sort out. Simply because being a tenant is both costly and sometimes a little complex, a little experienced advice will often help to avoid or resolve problems.

We are able to offer readers a practical problem-solving service. This telephone helpline service is available from 9 a.m. to 5 p.m., Monday to Friday, and the price is twenty-five pounds per year.

Tenants wishing to subscribe to this inexpensive service should contact us at Ethiclet Ltd, tel. 020 8942 0041, or email PL@Letting.Force9.co.uk.

Index